THE FEDERALIST WITHOUT TEARS

Jean Stearns

University Press
of America™

"*The Federalist* is not only a practical political document;
it is also an unsurpassed compendium of political truth."

Hans Morgenthau

"There is no better access to the flavor of the political
thinking of that age, to the subordination of ideological
to practical problems, and to the importance of constitu-
tionalism, than through the pages of *The Federalist*..."

Daniel J. Boorstin

Historian + Library of Cong.

"Hamilton, Madison, and Jay expounded the most serious
political thought of the times in the Federalist Papers
without for a moment renouncing party conflict or turn-
ing their backs on power."

Arthur Schlesinger

"To enumerate all the features of *The Federalist* that com-
mend it to citizens concerned with government and liberty
in the United States or the world would be to repeat many
pages and numbers of the work. But, in brief, it may be
safely said that there is scarcely a problem or aspect of
government which excites contemporary interest that is
left untouched in this great work."

Charles A. Beard

"FOR IN POLITICS, AS IN RELIGION, IT IS EQUALLY ABSURD
TO AIM AT MAKING PROSELYTES BY FIRE AND SWORD."

ALEXANDER HAMILTON

CONTENTS

PREFATORY NOTE

"Admittedly mastery of *The Federalist*
is not easy..." Charles A. Beard

Why would anyone want to tamper with *The Federalist Papers*?
My answer is brief. I can only hope it is sensible as well.

There are three primary documents which, taken together,
constitute the foundation of the American governmental system:
The Declaration of Independence, the Constitution, and *The Federalist
Papers*. The first document pronounced American independence; the
second gave substance to that pronouncement; the third gave to
America and the world the ablest defense and explanation of what was
achieved in Philadelphia.

The importance of these documents is seldom protested. But the
importance alone of *The Federalist* would hardly justify the attempt
to rewrite and summarize them. The justification (if there is any)
lies in the fact that the eighteenth century prose in which the Papers
are written is difficult--so difficult that many readers abandon them
after one paragraph.

The fault is not the reader's--nor can we blame Hamilton, Madison,
and Jay. It is something like the Wellfleet oyster--some say the best
in the world, but getting at one takes patience, a few tools and, on
occasion, it will not yield its succulence to any effort. However,
once it has been tasted, some people will go to any lengths to get
at one.

And so, sometime ago it came to me (by way of encouragement from
students, family, and friends) that it might not be altogether futile

3

to sacrifice the language of the authors to a simpler expression of what they had to say. The twenty-six Papers rewritten in contemporary language cover the major subject headings listed in the Table of Contents. Any selection is to some degree arbitrary, but I have tried to include those Papers that set forth the basic principles incorporated in the Constitution and that discuss the issues and problems that are pertinent to any study of modern political institutions.

The seven original Papers I selected for inclusion in this book treat the recurring themes and subjects of the complete *Federalist:* The nature of representative democracy, the meaning of faction and how to deal with it, the definition and discussion of federalism, and the structure and powers of the national government. These seven Papers are also representative of the tone and style of Hamilton, Madison, and Jay. The 85th and final Paper is simpler in language and organization, and because I want *Publius* to have the last word I have let *Federalist 85* stand by itself.

I hope that this "sampler" of *The Federalist* will whet your appetite--that you will want to go on to the others, that you will feel comfortable with them--that you will turn to them, not as part of an odious assignment, but for increased understanding of issues and problems that challenged the framers of our government and, with equal force, challenge us today.

Jean Stearns
Lieutenant Island
Wellfleet, Mass.
October 1976

INTRODUCTION

The American Constitution, the government it established, and *The Federalist* all owe their existence to men who refused to follow orders. The men who assembled in Philadelphia May 25, 1787, were instructed by a congressional resolution to establish "a firm national government,"--but they were not authorized to bring about that government by any means their collective wits could devise. The Resolution of Congress (passed February 21, 1787), was specific:

> Whereas there is provision in the Articles of Confederation & perpetual Union for making alteration therein by the Assent of a Congress of the United States and of the several States; And whereas experience hath evinced that there are defects in the present Confederation, as a means to remedy which several of the States, and particularly the State of New York by express instruction to their delegates in Congress have suggested a convention for the purposes expressed in the following resolution and such Convention appearing to be the most probable means of establishing in these states a firm national government.
>
> Resolved that in the opinion of Congress it is expedient that on the second Monday in May next a Convention of delegates who shall have been appointed by the several states be held at Philadelphia <u>for the sole and express purpose of revising the Articles of Confederation and reporting to Congress and the several legislatures such alterations and provisions therein as shall when agreed to in Congress and confirmed by the states render the federal constitution adequate to the exigencies of Government & the preservation of the Union</u>. (emphasis added)[1]

Four months later, however, thirty-nine men put their signatures to a brand new plan of government. Who were these men, and what did they do? There are many answers to that question. We can begin with the classic "textbook" explanation. It goes something like this: "these men who assembled in Philadelphia one hundred and eighty-nine years ago were not ordinary men. Jefferson, who then was Foreign Minister in France, referred to them as 'demi-

gods.' If they were not exactly demi-gods, they were, at the very
least, extraordinary--for the most part, young, widely experienced
in government, diplomacy, law, or business--all of them brilliant
and dedicated to the young nation. Among them were governors,
members of the Confederation Congress, signers of the Declaration
of Independence, and George Washington, who presided over the Convention was the very Father of the country, the personification of
American independence. And almost equally famous was the grand
patriarch of American politics and diplomacy, Ben Franklin. Franklin, though old and sick with gout, played grand conciliator; he
subdued the heated arguments and cooled the hot tempers. Because
he was too feeble to speak effectively, he often wrote down what
he wished to say and his words were read by other delegates.[2]
Never again would so many luminaries gather in one place to deliberate the government of this or any other nation..."

We read on, not exactly enthralled, but dutifully--we are informed that the Constitution consists of a "bundle of compromises,"
and we are introduced to them, one by one--the Virginia Plan, the
New Jersey Plan, the Three-Fifths Compromise, etc. We see them in
there, these framers, hot and sweaty, agreeing and diagreeing, ar-
guing and compromising, writing our Constitution. It seems to us
that they never ate or slept or left that hall, and besides, we are
trying to keep it all straight, those compromises, those "checks
and balances," the separation of power doctrine, this representative form of government they were building with words. They seem,
these men, to consist of nothing but quill pens and parchment. We
have almost forgotten why they were there, but--ah, here it is,
all reviewed for us--and in the nick of time. We are reminded that
only eleven years had passed since the Revolution. That war, exciting as it may have been, had drained the economy (always it is
"drained"), cut off commerce with Great Britain, pitted state
against state, debtor against creditor, the latter so violent an
affair that one desperate debtor, Shays of Massachusetts, resorted
to armed insurrection.[3] Congress, under the Articles of Confedera-

6

tion, lacked sufficient powers to govern. The demoralization, both economic and political, had resulted in deep hostility to all government. The national government (the very government that sent the men to Philadelphia) existed in name only--unable to tax, unable to provide for the nation's defense, unable to uphold the treaty of peace with Great Britain. There was no president and no national court system. Under those circumstances, is it any wonder that they "scrapped" (always it is "scrapped") the Articles and began anew? By this time we most certainly know that lesser men might not have been able to choose between the goal they were to achieve (a firm national government) and the means by which they were supposed to achieve that goal (altering the Articles of Confederation).

But that is not all; we continue to read. Drafting an entirely new instrument of government, against express instructions to the contrary, was indeed an act of boldness. But these men in Philadelphia went even further. Having done what they did, they knew it would be disastrous to submit their draft Constitution to the Congress and all thirteen states legislatures for approval; yet they were well aware the Article XIII of the Articles clearly stated that any change in the government was to be agreed upon by the Congress of the United States and ratified by the legislatures of every state. Having gone as far as they had, and not wanting to see their labors reduced to a mere forensic exercise, they changed the rules once again: they recommended to Congress that their Constitution be submitted to conventions held in each state and that, in addition, the new government should go into effect if and when it should be ratified by nine (not all) of the thirteen states.

The rest, you say, you know. Perhaps. We now have our Constitution and our Founding Fathers. Can we not leave well-enough alone? I suppose we can, but over here, to our left, is another book. We may as well have a look at it. What in the world is all this?..."The Founding Fathers (at least the term is familiar) were

7

indeed brilliant and talented men; they worked long and hard, but it is time to lay aside our childish naivete; let us look at them straight-on. They knew what they were doing, to be sure, but they looked out, first and last, for their own propertied and monied interests. They were elitists, every last one. Here are the charts and graphs to prove it--we can see their holdings in land and property. They wanted (and they wrote the plan) a government that would protect their wealth. The people? They distrusted them or, at the very best, 'the people, maybe.'" The Founding Fathers were, in short, the "nation's first elite."[4]

From demigods to elitists--from democrats to aristocrats-- from able and practical politicians to shrewd manipulators. There is a saying, "we cannot have it all ways," but in this case I think we can; in fact, I think we must. But more of this a little later. Let us return to less theoretical matters.

These fifty-five men from twelve states (Rhode Island refused to send any delegates) began their deliberations on May 25, 1787; on the last day of the Convention, September 17, 1787, forty-two were present and thirty-nine signed the draft Constitution. What happened to sixteen of the original fifty-five? Some left the sessions because of ill health or business affairs at home, but others (notably Robert Yates and John Lansing of New York) left in disgust, convinced that the Convention was in the process of exceeding its powers and subverting the government.[5] Though the delegates met in secret, behind closed doors, inevitably news leaked out;[6] the delegates wrote letters to family and friends and, of course, those who bolted were only too eager to alert their friends to what was taking place. For example, Yates and Lansing, in a great state of agitation, reported to Governor George Clinton of New York the facts of the matter as they saw them, condemning, in particular, what they viewed as the outrageous nationalist position taken by Hamilton, the third delegate from that state. Clinton, an opponent of strong national government, was quite frankly alarmed; he began at once to mobilize opposition to what he knew would be a

8

disastrous plan of government.[7] And so, the delegates who left
Philadelphia with their new and unauthorized scheme of government,
and a radical and unauthorized plan for its adoption, were far
from finished. What followed was a ten month national debate of
gigantic proportions. That debate, in large part, took place in
the press, both sides writing passionately and anonymously. It
was a fantastic war of words, many of those words long since buried in obscure and erudite books and documents. Letters for and
against the Constitution,[8] signed with such names as "Cato,"
"Sydney," "Agrippa," "Cassius," "A Landholder," (and others) began
appearing regularly in the newspapers of many states. Easily the
most famous series of letters in support of the Constitution appeared under pseudonym, "Publius." The first letter of this
series appeared in the *Independent Journal*, a New York newspaper,
on October 27, 1787. Eighty-four others followed.

The authorship of the letters may have been guessed before,
but it was not until 1792, five years after they were written,
that public announcement came: they were the joint enterprise of
Hamilton, Madison, and Jay. By this time, the letters had been
collected and printed in book form. Between the covers of a book,
the letters signed "Publius" became known as *The Federalist*.[9]

From the beginning the supporters of the Constitution called
themselves Federalists. The opponents of the Constitution were
furious; they considered themselves the <u>true</u> Federalists and felt
that the advocates of the new government were better called consol-
idationists or nationalists--even traitors, some felt, would not
be too strong. After all, they reasoned, the Constitution succeeded in establishing a strong national government by robbing the
states of power. A Federalist, they thought, stood for a more
equal division of power between the states and a central government. At any rate, they were too late; since those who supported
the Constitution called themselves Federalists, those who opposed
it were saddled with the name "anti-Federalist." "What's in a
name?" Well, sometimes a good deal.

9

Publius was Hamilton's brainchild. He knew that opposition to the Constitution, under the leadership of Governor Clinton, was especially strong in his home state of New York. He knew further that Yates and Lansing, the two New York delegates who bolted the Convention in its early stages, had launched a well planned campaign against ratification. Hamilton knew that the battle would be bitter and that already the Federalists were behind in their efforts.

It is interesting, curious, really, that it was Hamilton who took the initiative in the struggle for ratification. He did not attend very many sessions in Philadelphia after the first few weeks (he was there on the last day) and, more important than that, he argued for a much stronger national government than the one produced by the delegates. As a matter of fact, in June (1787) he presented to the delegates his own plan for a new government (he favored, among other things, life tenure for the president) and, a little later on, he referred to the Constitution as that "frail fabric."[10] But, this "frail fabric" was better than nothing--and better, to be sure, than the Articles of Confederation. He determined to do all he could to win friends to the plan and secure ratification.

There is probably no more difficult figure in American history to discuss or to do justice to than Hamilton, this illegitimate West Indian. Almost always he is compared to Jefferson, in much the same way a parent brags about the gifted and successful child in order to soften the sorrow of the wayward one. The comparison, some people think, comes naturally; they were contemporaries, both were nation-builders, but because they differed in their politics and philosophy, there seems to be some compulsion to jab away at Hamilton in order to keep the reverence for Jefferson intact. That this is so is most unfortunate--for Hamilton, for us, and for that matter, for Jefferson; the latter is in no way diminished by the recognition of Hamilton's brilliance or his far-reaching effects on the American constitutional system.[11]

10

The "textbook" analysis of Hamilton generally centers around
the facts that he was a brilliant financier, wrote over half of
the *Federalist* papers, was the able first Secretary of the Treasury in Washington's administration, launched the Bank of the United
States, and died as a result of a tragic, if somewhat romantic,
duel with Burr.[12] He is a shadowy figure, emerging from those
shadows when we want straight talk and a political realism tem-
pered by republican principles. We want (and appreciate) Hamilton
when the Declaration of Independence is not enough, when the realization strikes that the principles enunciated there mean nothing
without a Constitution and a government to give them life.[13] We
do not find Hamilton at our national celebrations--you will search
in vain for him at a 4th of July picnic; that day, of course, belongs to Jefferson, but he is conspicuously absent from our other
public days as well. How easy, finally, to attach labels to our
historic figures in order to simplify a sense of the past. Thus
it is that Jefferson is our leading democrat, our champion of individual rights; he instructs us that "that government is best that
governs least"--and Hamilton?--not a democrat, but a nationalist,
not a champion of the people, but a power-hungry, self-styled aristocrat interested in the power and the glory of the nation. But
when the fireworks are over, or there are tough questions to be
answered, such as: "What is an impeachable offense?"--"What is
the meaning of executive privilege?"--"What is the function of the
courts?"--"What is judicial review?"--jurists and journalists,
sometimes the people too, turn to Hamilton.

It may be that some have seen reflected in Hamilton their own
secret, cynical thoughts, those thoughts they sense are "un-Ameri-
can" and undemocratic. What, for instance, can we make of Woodrow
Wilson's observation that Hamilton was "a great man but not a great
American?"[14] Can you imagine it said of Churchill that he was a
great man but not a great Englishman? Or De Gaulle--that he was a
great man but not a great Frenchman? Only an American can be un-
American!

11

It is also said of Hamilton that he loved his country more deeply than his countrymen. Now that remark comes closer to hitting the mark. If there is one word, one theme, running through Hamilton's writings, his Publius letters, it is energy--energy in public officials and energy in government. Energy, for Hamilton, is not unbridled force; energy flows out of a structure of government that recognizes the necessity of power. True, power can be abused, but if it is, we cannot solve the problem by abandoning its use. The briefest look at *Federalist 1* is enough to show us that Hamilton, perhaps more than any of the founders, believed in the future greatness of America; he believed that this nation could be one of power and strength, that such power and strength, far from corrupting the nation's purpose or the rights of individuals, alone could bring to realization the former and protect the latter. Dare we lay at Hamilton's feet the abuse of power and the betrayal of trust we have experienced in recent years?

In the very first paragraph of *Federalist 1* Hamilton alludes to the country as empire. Characteristically, he looks ahead; he "dips into the future" and sees the United States as a world power. We flinch a little; have we not had enough of America as superpower? Yes, but in 1788, America was vulnerable to European conquest and domination, not vice versa. It is true that there was sentiment against a strong central government, but among the reasons for this sentiment was not that such a government threatened the American reputation abroad. As a matter of fact, in the eighteenth and nineteenth centuries, the national purpose was viewed within the context of increasing power and prominence in the world.[15]

But Hamilton can speak for himself. Perhaps it is time to read him--and less about him. To my mind, Clinton Rossiter put it extremely well:

> It has also been popular to describe Hamilton as a man who believed almost nothing that he wrote in the name of Publius, as a clever lawyer who took on a case he knew to be weak and won it with arguments he knew to be false.

To a large extent, this is all a matter of subjective opinion that could be noted and passed over except for one large implication: that the searcher for the 'true principles' of Hamilton's politics must not look into *The Federalist* lest he find too reasonable, too republican, and too constitutional a man.[16]

Hamilton solicited Madison's aid in writing the series of letters, though he probably first asked both Gouverneur Morris, the well-known and active delegate to the Convention from Pennsylvania, and William Duer, an aristocrat and politician from New York.[17] We are fortunate that both men turned Hamilton down, for it is unlikely that any other man at the time was better qualified to defend and explain the Constitution.

The thirty-six year old James Madison took with him to Philadelphia an enviable reputation and vast political knowledge. He was considered a leading political figure in his home state of Virginia and in the country; he worked with Jefferson in the drafting of the Declaration of Independence, helped draft the Virginia constitution, and had been a member of the Confederation Congress. He missed very little, minutes only, of the Convention's meetings and turned his amazing energies to every important problem the delegates faced. Most incredible of all, and most valuable for us today, is that he kept an unofficial Journal of the Convention's proceedings (all in longhand, incidentally). This Journal (properly called *Notes of Debates in the Federal Convention of 1787 as Reported by James Madison*) can tell us a great deal about the framers, the political theories behind the Constitution, and certainly gives us tremendous insight into Madison's mind.

Did Hamilton and Madison disagree on significant political issues—were their theories of representative democracy at odds with each other? A case can be made that they did differ—and that these differences are reflected in the Papers. The scholars who take this point of view, notably Alpheus T. Mason, claim that *The Federalist* has a "split personality."[18] However, not everyone agrees. Andrew Hacker, for instance, has an interesting theory.

Hacker agrees with those scholars who see a difference in "direction and emphasis" between Madison and Hamilton, but he sees similarities as well. He views both men as republicans rather than democrats and points out that both took a pessimistic view of human nature. Hacker suggests that Hamilton's arguments are more cohesive than Madison's. Hamilton consistently argued for a strong Executive branch, increased prestige abroad, and stressed the importance of industrial growth at home. Madison, according to Hacker, was less sure of the merits of concentrated national power and was a greater advocate of states' rights; Madison, in short, was ambivalent concerning the role of the national government. Should it for example, act as referee among competing groups and factions or should it develop policies quite separate from any other governmental unit? Hacker indicates that we can find both arguments in Madison's Papers. He concludes by suggesting that the "split personality" was not Publius but rather James Madison himself.[19]

Hacker may have had *Federalist 10* in mind when he wrote of Madison's "split personality." The now famous Number 10 (Madison's first contribution to Publius) remained in relative obscurity until the publication in 1913 of Charles Beard's, *Economic Interpretation of the Constitution of the United States*. Beard's thesis is that the Constitution reconciled conflicting economic interests in favor of wealthy property owners; his book caused quite a stir and sent scholars scurrying to *The Federalist* in search for substantiation of his thesis. Many thought (and think) that they found this substantiation in Madison's discussion of "faction" (interest and pressure groups). It is interesting to speculate how *Federalist 10* would be interpreted if Madison had omitted his controversial line --"but the most common and durable source of factions has been the various and unequal distribution of property." Scholars have seized upon that remark in an attempt to prove a number of unflattering theories concerning the philosophy underlying the Constitution and *The Federalist*.[20] Generations of students are familiar

14

with this one line (and generally it is taken out of context), but remain in blissful ignorance that Madison also observed that "where no substantial occasion presents itself, the most frivolous and fanciful distinctions have been sufficient to kindle their (the people) unfriendly passions and excite their most violent conflict." Very curious, actually, is that Beard himself, writing thirty-five years after he published *Economic Interpretation of the Constitution of the United States*, urges Americans to read *The Federalist* because of its magnificent _political_ _realism_; he recommends it to those who "prefer knowledge to self-deception..." Beard is not in the least disturbed that Madison saw "the various and unequal distribution of property" as "the most common and durable source of factions," but Beard, unlike so many other historians, reminds us that Madison also observed that men quarreled and fought for many other reasons or no reasons at all except "the most frivolous and fanciful distinction."[21]

Perhaps it is the "realism" Beard refers to that disturbs some readers of *Federalist 10*. It might be more comforting to believe that holding different views or having different interests and being unequal in abilities does not divide people into conflicting groups, but certainly our experience instructs us otherwise.[22]

John Jay, a wealthy New York lawyer, wrote five of the Papers. Jay was not a delegate to the Convention. In 1787, he was serving as secretary of foreign affairs under the Confederation government. He, Franklin, and John Adams negotiated the Treaty of 1783, thereby establishing the independence of the United States. Though he wrote only five of the Papers, all but one dealing with international relations and the treaty-making powers of the Senate, his contribution was important because he enjoyed tremendous prestige. He became, incidentally, the first Chief Justice of the United States, resigning that office in 1795 to become Governor of New York.

15

Why Read *The Federalist* in 1977?

The *Federalist Papers* were written in haste by busy men. They were written hurriedly, but a great deal of thought was given to the topics discussed--and what a wealth of subjects! It would be extravagant to claim that every issue of constitutional government is touched upon, but if our concern is the future of popular government we can do no better than to begin with *The Federalist*. One look at the Papers is enough to elicit our admiration--they read as though long hours were spent writing them. Yet there must have been no time for proofreading, no time to polish them, and though they do not constitute a systematic treatise on government (nor were they intended to), are sometimes repetitious and contain some inconsistencies, they are learned and eloquent. You may be all too eager to admit this, to acknowledge the brilliance and importance of the Papers, but still ask why we should concern ourselves with eighty-five essays addressed to newspaper readers in 1787 and 1788. After all, you protest, the immediate aim of *The Federalist* was to win friends for the Constitution and help bring about ratification. Is that not rather ancient history to us today? In addition, you might continue, the Constitution *The Federalist* explains and defends is greatly changed--interpretation by the courts, by presidents and legislatures and public opinion, plus twenty-six amendments have almost completely transformed the original document.

Some of the changes are indeed far-reaching: *The Federalist* was written before the Bill of Rights was added; certainly the lack of a Bill of Rights was the most serious objection to the draft Constitution. Madison had made it clear that he was "bound in honor" to see to it that such a Bill of Rights was passed by Congress immediately after ratification and, on December 15, 1791, the first ten Amendments were ratified.

Today the president and vice-president are directly elected (Amendment 12, ratified July 27, 1804); Amendment 13 abolished slavery (ratified December 6, 1865); Amendment 15 enfranchised the blacks (ratified Fébruary 3, 1870); personal incomes are directly

taxed (Amendment 16, ratified February 3, 1913); since 1913 senators have been directly elected (Amendment 17); in 1920 women were
granted the right to vote (Amendment 19); presidents can only be
reelected once (Amendment 22, ratified February 27, 1951); the imposition of poll taxes in national primaries was abolished in 1964
(Amendment 24); the voting age was lowered to age eighteen in 1971
(Amendment 26). State governments, though certainly not abolished
as some anti-Federalists feared, are weak and often ineffective;
executive agreements are frequently substituted for treaties (executive agreements do not need senatorial confirmation); the Senate is not always a highly distinguished body but is generally today more liberal and responsive to social and urban problems than
the House. We are concerned, not with Congressional tyranny but
with Congressional weakness; we fear an "imperial" Presidency.
Political parties the framers so hoped would not develop have been
with us since Washington's administration. The 1976 presidential
election once again exposed the weaknesses in the Electoral College
system. Simple arithmetic shows that a shift of 2,677 votes in
Ohio and about 3,700 votes in Hawaii would have reversed the out-
come of the election; Ford would have won by two electoral votes
even though Jimmy Carter had an absolute popular majority of 51
percent and received over 1.7 million more votes than Gerald Ford.

Technological advance has thrown at the feet of the political
institutions problems of staggering import: decay of our cities
and the devastation of the natural environment, violence in our
streets and record crime rates, the depersonalization of human relationships, the meaning of work, poverty and racial tension, the
decline of public and private morality, the specter of nuclear war-
fare, governmental invasion of privacy, genetic engineering, the
right to live and the right to die, to name but a few. Certainly
we cannot turn to the Constitution or *The Federalist* for "answers"
or solutions to these and other problems. Why, then, return at
all to the intricate arguments and explanations one finds in *The
Federalist*?

17

The reason must be that *The Federalist* (though limited in scope) is much more than a defense of the Constitution, though that defense is so brilliant that its reputation could rest on that alone. But far more important, in fact the exciting thing about *The Federalist* is that ever so lightly buried under the arguments and defenses of the Constitution lies a philosophy of human nature, social and political institutions, and a brilliant theory of representative government and federalism. Most of all, the living spirit of *The Federalist* is its faith in the power of reason. The mind of man, Publius says, made the Constitution possible. Man, though considerably lower than the angels, is nevertheless capable of self-government and of establishing institutions that will nourish his freedom and his talents. *The Federalist* is the politics of optimism, not the politics of despair.

At a time when government and power are suspect, indeed a time when government and power are feared, a time when scholars write of the end of ideology and the national purpose, we have much to gain by letting *The Federalist* present its convictions to us.[23] No other writing on the American constitutional system speaks so persuasively, so realistically, concerning the uses to which power can and should be put.

NOTES

1. Max Farrand, *Records of the Federal Convention* (New Haven: Yale University Press, 1937, Vol. 11), pp. 665-666.

2. Franklin did speak from time to time and never more charmingly than on the last day of the Convention. Madison's Journal records the following: "Whilst the last members were signing it Doctr. Franklin looking towards the President's Chair, at the back of which a rising sun happened to be painted, observed to a few members near him, that Painters had found it difficult to distinguish in their art a rising from a setting sun. 'I have,' said he, 'often and often in the course of the Session, and the vicissitudes of my hope and fears as to its issue, looked at that behind the President without being able to tell whether it was rising or setting: But now at length I have the happiness to know that it is a rising and not a setting sun.'" Quoted in Farrand, Vol. II, p. 648.

3. Shays' Rebellion actually served Hamilton's purposes very well. It gave him the ammunition he was seeking to assail the Articles of Confederation and to insist upon the necessity of calling a Constitutional Convention in order to strengthen the central government.

   The Revolution had produced a sizeable debtor class in America; farmers owed money on their farms and were unable to pay off their debts. As a result sheriffs and tax collectors (representing the creditors) repossessed farms in several of the states. The most serious situation developed in Massachusetts, culminating in Shays' Rebellion. Daniel Shays, a veteran of the Revolution, organized and led a group of insurgents in a march on the courthouses in several western Massachusetts towns. This uprising was put down by an army raised and equipped with money contributed by the wealthy landowners and merchants of the state. The insurrection was quelled, but Hamilton made the most of the fact that the Continential Congress had stood by while the state troops took over. He was later to ask, in Federalist 21: "Who can determine what might have been the issue of her (Massachusetts) late convulsions, if the malcontents had been headed by a Caesar or by a Cromwell? Who can predict what effect a despotism, established in Massachusetts would have upon the liberties of New Hampshire or Rhode Island, of Connecticut or New York?"

   For an excellent discussion concerning the significance of Shays' Rebellion, see John C. Miller, *Alexander Hamilton: Por-*

trait in Paradox (New York: Harper & Row, 1959), pp. 131-150. For the argument that the framers were indeed frightened by the radical insurrections in many of the states, see Thomas Dye and Ziegler, *The Irony of Democracy* (Belmont, California: Wadsworth Publishing Co., Inc., 1970), p. 28.

There are numerous references to Shays' Rebellion in the literature of the period--particularly during the ratification controversy. This Rebellion is treated with emotion and, quite frequently, with humor. Very few "Letters to the Editor" today are as colorful. The following remarks were written by James Sullivan (who wrote under the pseudonym "Cassius") and published in *The Massachusetts Gazette*: "Some writers in Massachusetts have discovered such weakness, inconsistency and folly in their productions, that it discovers them to be entirely ignorant of the subject they pretend to discuss, and totally unacquainted with the plan of government proposed by the federal convention. Among this number, is a scribbler under the signature of Vox Populi, whose signature, to have been consistent with his productions, should have been Vox Insania. This pompous and very learned scribbler, goes on to harrangue the public about the danger, hazard, terrour and destruction which will attend the adoption of the federal Constitution. He pleads, in a mournful strain, much about woful experience. From this circumstance, I am induced to suppose Vox Populi was an adherent of the celebrated Shays, in his unfortunate expedition the last winter, and wofully experienced the misfortune attendant on the insurgents, through the energy of government. However, the inhabitants of Massachusetts may be assured, that they will have Woful Experience with a witness, if they suffer themselves to be led away by such ignorant, knavish and designing numbheads as Vox Populi and his clan, so far as to reject the plan of federal government proposed by the Convention." Quoted in Paul Leicester Ford (ed.), *Essays on the Constitution of the United States* (originally published Brooklyn, New York, 1892, reprinted New York: Burt Franklin, 1970), pp.12-13.

The letters signed, "Landholder" (published simultaneously in the *Connecticut Courant* at Hartford and the *American Mercury* at Litchfield) were written by Oliver Ellsworth, a member of the Convention. In a letter published December 3, 1787, he wrote: "A concurrence of circumstances frequently enables a few disaffected persons to make great revolutions, unless government is vested with the most extensive powers of self-defence. Had Shays, the malcontent of Massachusetts, been a man of genius, fortune and address, he might have conquered that state, and by the aid of a little sedition in the other states, and an army proud by victory, become the monarch and tyrant of America. Fortunately he was checked; but should jealousy prevent vesting these powers in the hands of men chosen by yourselves, and who are under every constitutional restraint, accident or design will in all probability raise up some future Shays to be the tyrant of your children." Ford, *Essays*, p. 157.

4. Several historians and political scientists take the position that the framers, though able men, were fundamentally elitists concerned with protecting property rights and their own financial interests. See especially Charles Beard, *An Economic Interpretation of the Constitution of the United States* (New York: Macmillan Co., 1913); Clinton Rossiter, *1787, The Grand Convention* (New York: Macmillan Co., 1966); Thomas Dye and Harmon Ziegler, *The Irony of Democracy* (Belmont, California: Wadsworth Publishing Co., Inc., 1970) and David Schuman, *A Preface to Politics* (Lexington, Massachusetts; D.C. Heath and Co., 1973).

5. For an excellent discussion of this point see Benjamin Fletcher Wright, (ed.), *The Federalist* (Cambridge, Massachusetts: Harvard University Press, 1961.) Introduction.

6. William Patterson, in a letter to one of the delegates, wrote: "Full of Disputation and noisy as the Wind, it is said, that you are afraid of the very Windows, and have a Man planted under them to prevent the Secrets and Doings from flying out." Quoted in Farrand, Vol. IV, p. 73.

7. Most historians agree that the anti-Federalist letters signed "Cato" were written by Clinton. These letters appeared in *The New York Journal.* I am quoting the first one (September 27, 1787) in its entirety to give a "flavor" of the anti-Federalist argument:
   To the Citizens of the State of New York:
   The Convention, who sat at Philadelphia, have at last delivered to Congress that system of general government, which they have declared best calculated to promote your safety and happiness as citizens of the United States. This system, though not handed to you formally by the authority of government, has obtained an introduction through divers channels; and the minds of you all, to whose observation it has come, have no doubt been contemplating it; and alternate joy, hope, or fear have preponderated, as it conformed to, or differed from, your various ideas of just government.
   Government, to an American, is the science of his political safety; this then is a moment to you the most important--and that in various points--to your immediate safety, and to that of your posterity. In your private concerns and affairs of life you deliberate with caution, and act with prudence; your public concerns require a caution and prudence, in a ratio suited to the difference and dignity of the subject. The disposal of your reputation, and of your lives and property, is more momentous than a contract

21

for a farm, or the sale of a bale of goods; in the former, if you are negligent or inactive, the ambitious and despotic will entrap you in their toils, and bind you with the cord of power from which you, and your posterity may never be freed; and if the possibility should exist, it carries along with it consequences that will make your community totter to its center: in the latter, it is the mere loss of a little property, which more circumspection or assiduity may repair.

Without directly engaging as an advocate for this new form of national government, or as an opponent--let me conjure you to consider this a very important crisis of your safety and character. You have already, in common with the rest of your countrymen, the citizens of the other states, given to the world astonishing evidence of your greatness--you have fought under peculiar circumstances, and were successful against a powerful nation on a speculative question, you have established an original compact between you and your governors, a fact heretofore unknown in the formation of the government of the world; your experience has informed you, that there are defects in the federal system, and, to the astonishment of mankind, your alteration now lies before you, for your consideration; but beware how you determine--do not, because you admit that something must be done, adopt anything--teach the members of that convention that you are capable of a supervision of their conduct. The same medium that gave you this system, if it is erroneous, while the door is now open, can make amendments, or give you another, if it is required. Your fate, and that of your posterity, depends on your present conduct; do not give the latter reason to curse you, nor yourselves cause of reprehension; as individuals you are ambitious of leaving behind you a good name, and it is the reflection that you have done right in this life, that blunts the sharpness of death; the same principles would be a consolation to you, as patriots, in the hour of dissolution, that you would leave to your children a fair political inheritance, untouched by the vultures of power, which you had acquired by an <u>unshaken perseverance</u> in the cause of liberty; but how miserable the alternative--you would deprecate the ruin you had brought upon yourselves, be the curse of posterity, and the scorn and scoff of nations.

Deliberate, therefore, on this new national government with coolness; analize it with criticism; and reflect on it with candor: if you find that the influence of a powerful few, or the exercise of a standing army, will always be directed and exerted for your welfare alone, and not to the aggrandizement of themselves, and that it will secure to you and your posterity happiness at home, and national dignity and respect from abroad, adopt it; if it will not,

reject it with indignation--better to be where you are for
the present, than insecure forever afterwards. Turn your
eyes to the United Netherlands, at this moment, and view
their situation; compare it with what yours may be, under
a government substantially similar to theirs.
Beware of those who wish to influence your passions,
and to make you dupes to their resentments and little in-
terests--personal invectives can never persuade, but they
always fix prejudices, which candor might have removed--
those who deal in them have not your happiness at heart.
Attach yourselves to measures, not to men.
This form of government is handed to you by the recom-
mendations of a man who merits the confidence of the public; but you ought to recollect that the wisest and best
of men may err, and their errors, if adopted, may be fatal
to the community; therefore, in principles of politics, as
well as in religious faith, every man ought to think for
himself.
Hereafter, when it will be necessary, I shall make such
observations on this new constitution as will tend to promote your welfare and be justified by reason and truth.
Quoted in Ford, Essays, pp. 247-249.

8. Before the Publius letters were written, there appeared in
    the New York paper, The Daily Advertiser, several letters in
    support of the Constitution. These letters were signed
    "Caesar." Most scholars including Paul Leicester Ford, attri-
    bute these letters to Hamilton. Two points are certain: the
    letters were in answer to "Cato," and they struck a very abra-
    sive and insulting tone--insulting, that is, to the intelli-
    gence of the American newspaper readers. In recent years,
    however, scholars have suggested that Hamilton was not the au-
    thor. I tend to support this contention. Hamilton was too
    smart to deliberately insult his readers. The "Caesar" let-
    ters can be found in Ford's Essays, pp. 283-291. For the ar-
    gument that Hamilton was not the author of these letters, see
    especially Jacob E. Cooke, "Alexander Hamilton's Authorship
    of the 'Caesar' Letters," William and Mary Quarterly, 3rd
    Series, XVII, No. 1 (Jan., 1960), pp. 78-85.

9. There is still some dispute concerning the authorship of cer-
    tain Papers. One problem is that by the time the authorship
    was made public, Hamilton and Madison no longer agreed with
    all the positions they had expressed in The Federalist. This
    was embarrassing to them. Benjamin Fletcher Wright points
    out that had it not been for Hamilton's duel with Burr perhaps
    neither "of the chief authors of The Federalist would have
    made public their claims to authorship for many years. That
    fantastic affair, was representative of Hamilton's romantic

23

belief in glory and manly honor as his financial program was
representative of his zeal for national strength, caused him
to take measures to put his personal affairs in order and to
insure his lasting fame. Most curious was his placing in a
friend's bookcase, where it would certainly be found, a slip
of paper listing the authors of the various Publius letters."
Wright, *The Federalist*, p. 9. Hamilton, incidentally, claimed
many more papers than most scholars think he wrote. I have
taken the assignment of authorship given by Benjamin Fletcher
Wright, who took his from Douglass Adair. See Adair, "The
Authorship of the Disputed Federalist Papers," *William and
Mary Quarterly*, 3rd Series, I (1944), pp. 97-122, 235-264.

10. See Farrand, *Records*, Vol. III, pp. 617-630.

11. In a letter to James Madison, dated November 18, 1788, Jefferson had this to say of *The Federalist*: "I read it with care,
pleasure and improvement, and was satisfied that there was
nothing in it by one of those (three) hands, and not a great
deal by a second. It does honor to the third, as being, in
my opinion, the best commentary on the principles of government which was ever written." *The Writings of Thomas Jefferson*, A. Bergh (ed.), Vol. VII, (Washington D.C., 1905), p. 183.
Jefferson may have thought at the time that Madison was the
chief author of *The Federalist*. Would he have written as he
did had he known Hamilton wrote over half the Papers?
    Charles Beard, who certainly viewed the framers without
sentiment, cautioned his readers against political bias concerning Hamilton. He wrote that we ought to ask ourselves
what might have happened to the country or to the Constitution
if Hamilton had not lived or worked so hard to support both.
See Charles Beard, *The Enduring Federalist* (New York: Doubleday & Company, Inc., 1948), pp. 10-11.

12. For an interesting insight into Hamilton's attitude towards
Burr, see Broadus Mitchell, *Heritage from Hamilton* (New York:
Columbia Univ. Press, 1957), pp. 140-152.

13. Writers who argue that the framers were elitists and that they
were in no way interested in establishing a democratic form of
government also claim that the philosophy of the Declaration
of Independence was killed in Philadelphia. Fortunately there
are other scholars in our midst who effectively counter this
argument. Adrienne Koch, for example, wrote that the burden
of proof falls upon those who deliberately "twist" the Convention into a philosophically false opposition to the "spirit of
'76." The important right of a free people "to institute new

24

Government, laying its foundation on such principles and organizing its powers in such a form, as to them shall seem
most likely to effect their Safety and Happiness" is certainly
the central core of the Declaration. This mandate was carried
out in Philadelphia. In addition, one look at the Constitution and *The Federalist* leaves no doubt that the ultimate
source of political authority and power resides in the people.
See Adrienne Koch (ed.), *Notes of Debates in the Federal Convention of 1787 Reported by James Madison* (Athens, Ohio: Ohio
University Press, 1966), xvii-xix. See also Wright (ed.), *The
Federalist*, p. 22.

14. Woodrow Wilson, *The New Freedom* (New York: Doubleday, Page &
Co., 1913), p. 55. Curiously, toward the end of the book,
Wilson wrote the following: "What is liberty? I have long
had an image in my mind of what constitutes liberty. Suppose
that I were building a great piece of powerful machinery, and
suppose that I should so awkwardly and unskilfully assemble
the parts of it that every time one part tried to move it
would buckle up and be checked. Liberty for the several parts
would consist in the best possible assembling and adjustment
of them all, would it not? If you want the great piston of
the engine to run with absolute freedom, give it absolutely
perfect alignment and adjustment with the other parts of the
machine, so that it is free, not because it has been associa-
ted most skilfully and carefully with the other parts of the
great structure.
    "What is liberty? You say of the locomotive that it runs
free. What do you mean? You mean that its parts are so assembled and adjusted that friction is reduced to a minimum,
and that it has perfect adjustment. We say of a boat skimming
the water with light foot, 'How free she runs,' when we mean,
how perfectly she is adjusted to the force of the wind, how
perfectly she obeys the great breath out of the heavens that
fill her sails. Throw her head up into the wind and see how
she will halt and stagger, how every sheet will shiver and her
whole frame be shaken, how instantly she is 'in irons,' in the
expressive phrase of the sea. She is free only when you have
let her fall off again and have recovered once more her nice
adjustment to the forces she must obey and cannot defy. Human freedom consists in perfect adjustment of human interests
and human activities and human energies." Wilson, *The New
Freedom*, pp. 282-283. How like Hamilton he sounds!

15. Hans Morgenthau has pointed out that the "purpose" of America
has become blurred or ambiguous. What America stands for,
how this nation differs from other nations--these and similar
questions have in large part been abandoned. See Hans Morgenthau, *The Purpose of American Politics* (New York: Vintage

Books, 1964), p. 4. Daniel Boorstin argues (in a brilliant essay) that Americans are not interested in re-formulating the nation's purpose and are unconcerned with political philosophy because they believe that the framers, in one fell swoop, "handed" to us the perfect theory of popular government. See Daniel Boorstin, *The Genius of American Politics* (Chicago: University of Chicago Press, 1953), pp. 8-35.

16. Clinton Rossiter, *Alexander Hamilton and the Constitution* (New York: Harcourt, Brace & World, Inc., 1964), p. 59.

17. Hamilton, though born illegitimate, fashioned himself an aristocrat and, whenever possible, surrounded himself by the well-born. This may explain why he asked Duer to write some of the Papers. Duer supported the Revolution, was chosen as delegate from New York to the Continental Congress, and was a signer of the Articles of Confederation. But these facts are probably less important than others in explaining his relationship to Hamilton. Duer was wealthy and a successful New York City business man and, in his mode of living, very much the aristocrat. A contemporary, describing a dinner at his house said: "Colonel Duer...lives in the style of a nobleman. I presume he had not less than fifteen different sorts of wine at dinner and after the cloth was removed." Quoted in *The Dictionary of American Biography* (New York: Scribner's, 1959, Vol. 6), p. 487.

18. Alpheus T. Mason, "The Federalist--A Split Personality," *American Historical Review*, LVII (1952), pp. 625-643.

19. Andrew Hacker (Introduction), *The Federalist Papers* (New York: Washington Square Press, 1964), xv.

20. Some political scientists see in *Federalist 10* a vitriolic and anti-democratic treatise. Madison, they feel, could not have taken a dimmer view of man. One author of a recent American government text states flatly that *Federalist 10* is an essay on "mistrust." He accuses Madison of asking that government be trusted to the people while at the same time expressing little or no faith *in* the people. This writer goes even further: Madison, he says, encourages gross materialism and views people as anti-political. He sees *Federalist 10* as a Machiavellian essay on how to "divide and conquer." See David Schuman, *A Preface to Politics* (Lexington, Massachusetts: D.C. Heath & Company, 1973), pp. 18-19.

21. Beard, *The Enduring Federalist*, p. 15.

22. At any rate, Madison began a discussion on the meaning and significance of groups that has continued to the present. Theorists differ, of course, on the role of interest and pressure groups, as to whether or not they are valuable in policy formulation, whether or not they are important centers of power. Today scholars who accept Madison's analysis of factions (or groups) are called *pluralists*. Perhaps the best known advocate of pluralism is Robert A. Dahl. He, like Madison, believes that because one center of power is set against another, power will be controlled and no one group will become too dominant or coerce the others. Dahl's thesis is that the existence of many groups is the best guarantee that conflicts will be peacefully resolved. See Robert A. Dahl, *Pluralist Democracy in the United States* (Chicago: Rand McNally and Company, 1967), p. 24.

    The important question today, as it was in 1788, is where the power centers are. Not everyone agrees that power is (or can be) diffused among many groups; many political scientists believe it is concentrated in a *power elite*. Such an elite is comprised of people at the very top--in business, the military, and government. See especially C. Wright Mills, *The Power Elite* (New York: Oxford University Press, 1960).

23. See particularly Daniel Bell, *The End of Ideology* (New York: Collier Books, 1961) and Hans J. Morgenthau, *The Purpose of American Politics*.

27

BIBLIOGRAPHICAL NOTE

The Federalist is available in a number of editions. The first American edition, the McLean edition, was published in 1788; in 1886, G. P. Putnam's Sons published the Henry Cabot Lodge edition. These two early editions are considered authentic, but the Lodge edition contains many errors of typography and spelling. Another early (and well annotated) edition is Paul Leicester Ford's, published in 1898. The Benjamin Fletcher Wright edition (Cambridge, Mass.: The Belknap Press of Harvard University Press, 1961) is excellent; it is a faithful rendition of the McLean edition except for slight normalization of spelling. I have followed closely both the McLean and Wright editions and have provided my own titles for the rewritten Papers. It is interesting that the first public announcement of authorship came in the French edition (published in Paris in 1792). Charles A. Beard's edition, *The Enduring Federalist* (Garden City: Doubleday & Co., Inc., 1948) contains an informative introduction and Beard's own paragraph titles for the seventy-five Papers reprinted. The Papers collected and published in the 1788 edition, originally published in the New York newspapers *sereatim*, bore no titles of any kind. They were all addressed "To the People of the State of New York." There are many other editions; the most recent one, published by Robert B. Luce, Inc. (Washington-New York, 1976), closely follows the McLean edition but the table of contents is taken from the Henry Cabot Lodge edition.

HAMILTON

To the People of the State of New York:

After an unequivocal experience of the inefficiency of the subsisting federal government, you are called upon to deliberate on
a new Constitution for the United States of America. The subject
speaks its own importance; comprehending in its consequences nothing less than the existence of the UNION, the safety and welfare
of the parts of which it is composed, the fate of an empire in
many respects the most interesting in the world. It has been frequently remarked that it seems to have been reserved to the people
of this country, by their conduct and example, to decide the important question, whether societies of men are really capable or
not of establishing good government from reflection and choice,
or whether they are forever destined to depend for their political
constitutions on accident and force. If there be any truth in the
remark, the crisis at which we are arrived may with propriety be
regarded as the era in which that decision is to be made; and a
wrong election of the part we shall act may, in this view, deserve
to be considered as the general misfortune of mankind.

This idea will add the inducements of philanthropy to those
of patriotism, to heighten the solicitude which all considerate
and good men must feel for the event. Happy will it be if our
choice should be directed by a judicious estimate of our true interests, unperplexed and unbiased by considerations not connected
with the public good. But this is a thing more ardently to be
wished than seriously to be expected. The plan offered to our deliberations affects too many particular interests, innovates upon
too many local institutions, not to involve in its discussion a
variety of objects foreign to its merits, and of views, passions
and prejudices little favorable to the discovery of truth.

Among the most formidable of the obstacles which the new Constitution will have to encounter may readily be distinguished the obvious interest of a certain class of men in every State to resist all changes which may hazard a diminution of the power, emolument, and consequence of the offices they hold under the State establishments; and the perverted ambition of another class of men, who will either hope to aggrandize themselves by the confusions of their country, or will flatter themselves with fairer prospects of elevation from the subdivision of the empire into several martial confederacies than from its union under one government.

It is not, however, my design to dwell upon observations of this nature, I am well aware that it would be disingenuous to resolve indiscriminately the opposition of any set of men (merely because their situations might subject them to suspicion) into interested or ambitious views. Candor will oblige us to admit that even such men may be actuated by upright intentions; and it cannot be doubted that much of the opposition which has made its appearance, or may hereafter make its appearance, will spring from sources, blameless at least, if not respectable--the honest errors of minds led astray by preconceived jealousies and fears. So numerous indeed and so powerful are the causes which serve to give a false bias to the judgment, that we, upon many occasions, see wise and good men on the wrong as well as on the right side of questions of the first magnitude to society. This circumstance, if duly attended to, would furnish a lesson of moderation to those who are ever so much persuaded of their being in the right in any controversy. And a further reason for caution, in this respect, might be drawn from the reflection that we are not always sure that those who advocate the truth are influenced by purer principles than their antagonists. Ambition, avarice, personal animosity, party opposition, and many other motives not more laudable than these, are apt to operate as well upon those who support as those who oppose the right side of a question. Were there not even inducements to moderation, nothing could be more ill-judged than that

30

intolerant spirit which has, at all times, characterized political parties. For in politics, as in religion, it is equally absurd to aim at making proselytes by fire and sword. Heresies in either can rarely be cured by persecution.

And yet, however just these sentiments will be allowed to be, we have already sufficient indications that it will happen in this as in all former cases of great national discussion. A torrent of angry and malignant passions will be let loose. To judge from the conduct of the opposite parties, we shall be led to conclude that they will mutually hope to evince the justness of their opinions, and to increase the number of their converts by the loudness of their declamations and the bitterness of their invectives. An enlightened zeal for the energy and efficiency of government will be stigmatized as the offspring of a temper fond of despotic power and hostile to the principles of liberty. An over-scrupulous jealousy of danger to the rights of the people, which is more commonly the fault of the head than of the heart, will be represented as mere pretence and artifice, the stale bait for popularity at the expense of the public good. It will be forgotten, on the one hand, that jealousy is the usual concomitant of love, and that the noble enthusiasm of liberty is apt to be infected with a spirit of narrow and illiberal distrust. On the other hand, it will be equally forgotten that the vigor of government is essential to the security of liberty; that, in the contemplation of a sound and well-informed judgment, their interest can never be separated; and that a dangerous ambition more often lurks behind the specious mask of zeal for the rights of the people than under the forbidding appearance of zeal for the firmness and efficiency of government. History will teach us that the former has been found a much more certain road to the introduction of despotism than the latter, and that of those men who have overturned the liberties of republics, the greatest number have begun their career by paying an obsequious court to the people; commencing demagogues, and ending tyrants.

In the course of the preceding observations, I have had an eye, my fellow-citizens, to putting you upon your guard against all attempts, from whatever quarter, to influence your decision in a matter of the utmost moment to your welfare, by any impressions other than those which may result from the evidence of truth. You will, no doubt, at the same time, have collected from the general scope of them, that they proceed from a source not unfriendly to the new Constitution. Yes, my countrymen, I own to you that, after having given it an attentive consideration, I am clearly of opinion it is your interest to adopt it. I am convinced that this is the safest course for your liberty, your dignity, and your happiness. I affect not reserves which I do not feel. I will not amuse you with an appearance of deliberation when I have decided. I frankly acknowledge to you my convictions, and I will freely lay before you the reasons on which they are founded. The consciousness of good intentions disdains ambiguity. I shall not, however, multiply professions on this head. My motives must remain in the depository of my own breast. My arguments will be open to all, and may be judged of by all. They shall at least be offered in a spirit which will not disgrace the cause of truth.

I propose, in a series of papers, to discuss the following interesting particulars: -- *The utility of the UNION to your political prosperity* -- *The insufficiency of the present Confederation to preserve that Union* -- *The necessity of a government at least equally energetic with the one proposed, to the attainment of this object* -- *The conformity of the proposed Constitution to the true principles of republican government* -- *Its analogy to your own State constitution* -- and lastly, *The additional security which its adoption will afford to the preservation of that species of government, to liberty, and to property.*

In the progress of this discussion I shall endeavor to give a satisfactory answer to all the objections which shall have made their appearance, that may seem to have any claim to your attention.

It may perhaps be thought superfluous to offer arguments to
prove the utility of the UNION, a point, no doubt, deeply engraved
on the hearts of the great body of the people in every State, and
one, which it may be imagined, has no adversaries. But the fact
is, that we already hear it whispered in the private circles of
those who oppose the new Constitution, that the thirteen States
are of too great extent for any general system, and that we must
of necessity resort to separate confederacies of distinct portions
of the whole.* This doctrine will, in all probability, be gradually
propagated, till it has votaries enough to countenance an open
avowal of it. For nothing can be more evident, to those who are
able to take an enlarged view of the subject, than the alternative
of an adoption of the new Constitution or a dismemberment of the
Union. It will therefore be of use to begin by examining the advantages of that Union, the certain evils, and the probable dangers, to which every State will be exposed from its dissolution.
This shall accordingly constitute the subject of my next address.

PUBLIUS

----

   * The same idea, tracing the arguments to their consequences
is held out in several of the late publications against the new
Constitution. --PUBLIUS

HAMILTON

You have experienced the inefficiency of the present national government and are now being asked to consider a new Constitution. I
do not have to insist upon the importance of this subject; the very
existence of this most interesting nation, this empire, depends upon what we decide to do. We are in a unique position to answer the
most important of all political questions: is it possible for men
to deliberate together and to establish a good government by reason
and choice? If the answer is "yes," our action will have world-
wide significance.

But we must be realistic. Many people will oppose the Constitution because they feel their personal and business interests will
suffer under the new government. Very strong opposition will come
from men who hold political positions in the state governments;
they will fear loss of power and money. Some men will oppose the
Constitution because they hope to benefit by the present confusion;
others see their futures more successful in a nation permanently
divided into several states, rather than firmly united under one
national government.

I am not, however, going to dwell on the motives of those who
oppose the Constitution. To do so is too falsely clever and simple.
Quite frankly, some people who oppose the Constitution are motivated by honest and legitimate feelings. Others oppose the Constitution, not because they are evil or against the public good, but
because their judgment is unsound and their fears are groundless.
There are so many prejudices which can affect good judgment that
many times we find wise and good men on the wrong side of important
questions. This fact ought to sober those who think that they are
always right! We can add a further irony; some people will support
the Constitution for the wrong reasons; for example, some people

will hope to promote their own power and position under the new government.

Political controversies, like religious ones, are character-ized by passion and intolerance. Already the anti-Federalists are speaking and writing against the Constitution. The language they use is highly emotional and abusive. They hope to make it appear that those of us who favor the Constitution are unconcerned with the principles of liberty. Other extremists are sincerely afraid that the rights of the people are threatened by the proposed gov-ernment. This is the result of faulty thinking more than anything else. Their case will continue to be charged with emotion. Enthu-iastic supporters of liberty often think they see it threatened when, in fact, no threat exists. This is understandable. Lovers of liberty, like all lovers, are jealous and protective. Unfor-tunately, such passion for liberty prevents men from realizing that unless government is strong, liberty is insecure. To advocate vig-orous and efficient government lacks emotional appeal, but history teaches us that to cherish liberty in the absence of strong govern-ment often results in despotism. Some political leaders conceal dangerous personal ambitions by talking endlessly about the "rights of the people;" these leaders begin as rabble-rousers and end up as tyrants.

Even though what I have said stands the test of history and experience, you may still have doubts. It is obvious I seek your approval of the Constitution. I am convinced that it is in your interest to adopt it, for it will best preserve your liberty, dig-nity, and happiness. I refuse to be coy; I will not attempt to amuse you by pretending that I am still deliberating when I have already decided. I am being candid about my convictions and will give you the reasons behind them. If one is really sincere, straight-forward arguments should be presented. My motives for urging ratification of the Constitution are personal, but my argu-ments are open.

I propose, in a series of Papers, to discuss the following

35

specific issues raised by the new Constitution: (1) Your political prosperity and the Constitution; (2) The inadequacy of the present government to preserve the UNION; (3) The necessity of strong and energetic government; (4) The Constitution and its relationship to republican principles of government; (5) The similarity of the proposed Constitution to your own state constitution; (6) The protection of liberty and property under the proposed government.

I shall also try to effectively answer serious arguments brought against ratification.

You may think that it is unnecessary to plead for a strong Union, but the argument is heard that the country is too large to establish a national system of government. No doubt this argument will gain strength sufficient for its advocates to bring it out into the open and make the most of it. It seems to me that it comes down to this: either we adopt the Constitution or we will see the end of a united country.

In the next Paper we will examine the advantage of Union and the disadvantages and dangers to the states should the Union be dissolved.

The question before the American people is so important that all
citizens must give it their greatest attention.

We must begin with two facts of political life: some form of
government is necessary in a society, and all forms of government
must be granted sufficient power to regulate conflict and administer the laws. Who grants these powers? The people do. The
establishment of government itself implies that the people grant
to that government certain rights they formerly reserved to themselves. That being so, the American people must decide what form
of government will be most effective and best protect their interests. The choice is between uniting under one national government
or dividing into separate states, with each state governor possessing as much power as the Constitution advises placing in one
national government.

Until recently it was generally agreed that America's prosperity depends upon being firmly united, but some politicians now
argue that the country ought to be divided into sovereign states
with no central government at all. The number of people who think
this way is increasing. How do we answer this argument?

We are united in many natural ways. Even the geography of
this beautiful and fertile country suggests that we remain a united people. The states are connected by navigable streams and
rivers; these navigable waters encourage transportation of various
commodities from state to state and bind the country together. We
speak the same language, practice the same religion, and believe
in the same principles of government. We are similar in manners
and customs.

The most important reason to remain united is that we successfully fought a long and bloody war of independence. We were still

at war, our houses burning and our citizens bleeding, when the decision was made to form a national government. That government was hastily formed; the war did not allow time to deliberate. It is no wonder that this government is now unable to meet the demands of a growing nation. How fortunate we are that some intelligent people realized the necessity of framing a new national government. The Constitutional Convention was composed of extraordinary men who deliberated for four months, unawed by power and free from corrupting influences. Their remarkable plan reflects the quality of their deliberations.

It is significant that this plan is recommended to us--not imposed upon us. The framers do not ask for blind acceptance. They want sober consideration, equal to the imporance of the subject. But our experience indicates that some people, motivated by prejudices and selfish interests, will speak out against the proposed government. In the end, however, the people will put their trust and confidence in it, just as they finally supported the Congress of 1774. The men in the Congress of 1774 were relatively unknown and untested; the men who framed this government are widely experienced and nationally prominent.

It seems to me that the majority of the people and the present Congress favor the proposed government under the new Constitution. That some men in our midst want the country broken up into separate confederacies should not discourage us from doing all we can to strengthen this great country.

9

HAMILTON

The states will be more stable under a strong national government because such a government will be able to repress lawlessness and insurrection. For those people who know their ancient history this point is difficult to accept; they read that the old Greek and Italian republics were marked by revolutions and political instability, and they conclude that all popular government is inconsistent with a well-ordered society. We will consider this argument.

If it had proved impossible or impractical to devise model forms of republican government, or if history revealed none, men would be justified in abandoning republicanism, or representative democracy, as a workable structure of government. Many, but not all, ancient republics were indeed corrupt and unstable; however, in recent years the art and science of politics have improved considerably. The four major advances in the republican theory of government are: (1) the division of power among the branches of government; (2) the introduction of legislative "checks" on executive power; (3) the establishment of an independent judicial branch; and, (4) the election of representatives to the legislative branch. These four principles make a significant difference in the evaluation of the republican form of government. I would like to suggest a fifth principle which, interestingly enough, is often used as an argument against adopting the new government. It is this: the republican form of government operates more, not less, effectively in a large country.

This is not a particularly new idea, yet there is tremendous opposition to it. I think the opposition stems, in large part, from those people who read small portions of Montesquieu's work (the great French political theorist). Montesquieu, in some of

39

his writing, does seem to suggest that republican government is not suited to large countries, that such a form is too cumbersome, but in certain other writings of his we find arguments that would support republican government in a country the size of ours. There is nothing in Montesquieu's writings that suggests that states should not be bound together under one central government. As a matter of fact, he explicitly suggests a confederate republic as the solution for "extending the sphere of popular government, and reconciling the advantages of monarchy with those of republicanism." Montesquieu's argument also supports my contention that the government set up by the Constitution will tend to repress domestic faction and insurrection.

Some opponents of the Constitution claim that the proposed government ignores the principles of confederacy and establishes a consolidation of the states. The difference between confederation and consolidation is subtle--more a matter of semantics than anything else. At any rate, the Constitution does not, in any way, propose the abolition of state governments. On the contrary, the states will have direct and equal representation in the Senate and will retain certain exclusive and important powers. The position and powers the states will enjoy under the new government conform with the principles of federalism.

MADISON

To the People of the State of New York:

Among the numerous advantages promised by a well-constructed Union, none deserves to be more accurately developed than its tendency to break and control the violence of faction. The friend of popular governments never finds himself so much alarmed for their character and fate, as when he contemplates their propensity to this dangerous vice. He will not fail, therefore, to set a due value on any plan which, without violating the principles to which he is attached, provides a proper cure for it. The instability, injustice, and confusion introduced into the public councils, have, in truth, been the mortal diseases under which popular governments have everywhere perished; as they continue to be the favorite and fruitful topics from which the adversaries to liberty derive their most specious declamations. The valuable improvements made by the American constitutions on the popular models, both ancient and modern, cannot certainly be too much admired; but it would be an unwarrantable partiality, to contend that they have as effectually obviated the danger on this side, as was wished and expected. Complaints are everywhere heard from our most considerate and virtuous citizens, equally the friends of public and private faith, and of public and personal liberty, that our governments are too unstable, that the public good is disregarded in the conflicts of rival parties, and that measures are too often decided, not according to the rules of justice and the rights of the minor party, but by the superior force of an interested and overbearing majority. However anxiously we may wish that these complaints had no foundation, the evidence of known facts will not permit us to deny that they are in some degree true. It will be found, indeed, on a candid review of our situation, that some of the distresses under which we labor have been erroneously charged on the operation of our governments; but it will be found, at the same time, that other causes will not alone account for many of our heaviest misfortunes; and, particularly, for that prevailing and increasing distrust of public engagements, and alarm for private rights, which are echoed from one end of the continent to the other. These must be chiefly, if not wholly, effects of the unsteadiness and injustice with which a factious spirit has tainted our public administrations.

By a faction, I understand a number of citizens, whether amounting to a majority or minority of the whole, who are united and actuated by some common impulse of passion, or of interest, adverse to the rights of other citizens, or to the permanent and aggregate interests of the community.

There are two methods of curing the mischiefs of faction: the one, by removing its causes; the other, by controlling its effects.

There are again two methods of removing the causes of faction: the one, by destroying the liberty which is essential to its existence; the other, by giving to every citizen the same opinions, the same passions, and the same interests.

It could never be more truly said than of the first remedy, that it was worse than the disease. Liberty is to faction what air is to fire, an aliment without which it instantly expires. But it could not be less folly to abolish liberty, which is essential to political life, because it nourishes faction, than it would be to wish the annihilation of air, which is essential to animal life, because it imparts to fire its destructive agency.

The second expedient is as impracticable as the first would be unwise. As long as the reason of man continues fallible, and he is at liberty to exercise it, different opinions will be formed. As long as the connection subsists between his reason and his self-love, his opinions and his passions will have a reciprocal influence on each other: and the former will be objects to which the latter will attach themselves. The diversity in the faculties of

42

men, from which the rights of property originate, is not less an insuperable obstacle to a uniformity of interests. The protection of these faculties is the first object of government. From the protection of different and unequal faculties of acquiring property, the possession of different degrees and kinds of property immediately results; and from the influence of these on the sentiments and views of the respective proprietors, ensues a division of the society into different interests and parties.

The latent causes of faction are thus sown in the nature of man; and we see them everywhere brought into different degrees of activity, according to the different circumstances of civil society. A zeal for different opinions concerning religion, concerning government, and many other points, as well of speculation as of practice; an attachment to different leaders ambitiously contending for pre-eminence and power; or to persons of other descriptions whose fortunes have been interesting to the human passions, have, in turn, divided mankind into parties, inflamed them with mutual animosity, and rendered them much more disposed to vex and oppress each other than to co-operate for their common good. So strong is this propensity of mankind to fall into mutual animosities, that where no substantial occasion presents itself, the most frivolous and fanciful distinctions have been sufficient to kindle their unfriendly passions and excite their most violent conflicts. But the most common and durable source of factions has been the various and unequal distribution of property. Those who hold and those who are without property have ever formed distinct interests in society. Those who are creditors, and those who are debtors, fall under a like discrimination. A landed interest, a manufacturing interest, a mercantile interest, a moneyed interest with many lesser interests, grow up of necessity in civilized nations, and divide them into different classes, actuated by different sentiments and views. The regulation of these various and interfering interests forms the principal task of modern legislation, and involves the spirit of party and faction in the necessary and ordi-

43

nary operations of the government.

No man is allowed to be a judge in his own cause, because his interest would certainly bias his judgment, and, not improbably, corrupt his integrity. With equal, nay with greater reason, a body of men are unfit to be both judges and parties at the same time; yet what are many of the most important acts of legislations, but so many judicial determinations, not indeed, concerning the rights of single persons, but concerning the rights of large bodies of citizens? And what are the different classes of legislators but advocates and parties to the causes which they determine? Is a law proposed concerning private debts? It is a question to which the creditors are parties on one side and the debtors on the other. Justice ought to hold the balance between them. Yet the parties are, and must be, themselves the judges; and the most numerous party, or, in other words, the most powerful faction must be expected to prevail. Shall domestic manufactures be encouraged, and in what degree, by restrictions on foreign manufactures? are questions which would be differently decided by the landed and the manufacturing classes, and probably by neither with a sole regard to justice and the public good. The apportionment of taxes on the various ous descriptions of property is an act which seems to require the most exact impartiality; yet there is, perhaps, no legislative act in which greater opportunity and temptation are given to a predominant party to trample on the rules of justice. Every shilling with which they overburden the inferior number, is a shilling saved to their own pockets.

It is in vain to say that enlightened statesmen will be able to adjust these clashing interests, and render them all subservient to the public good. Enlightened statesmen will not always be at the helm. Nor, in many cases, can such an adjustment be made at all without taking into view indirect and remote considerations, which will rarely prevail over the immediate interest which one party may find in disregarding the rights of another or the good of the whole.

44

The inference to which we are brought is, that the *causes* of faction cannot be removed, and that relief is only to be sought in the means of controlling its *effects*.

If a faction consists of less than a majority, relief is supplied by the republican principle, which enables the majority to defeat its sinister views by regular vote. It may clog the administration, it may convulse the society; but it will be unable to execute and mask its violence under the forms of the Constitution. When a majority is included in a faction, the form of popular government, on the other hand, enables it to sacrifice to its ruling passion or interest both the public good and the rights of other citizens. To secure the public good and private rights against the danger of such a faction, and at the same time to preserve the spirit and the form of popular government, is then the great object to which our inquiries are directed. Let me add that it is the great desideratum by which this form of government can be rescued from the opprobrium under which it has so long labored, and be recommended to the esteem and adoption of mankind.

By what means is this object attainable? Evidently by one of two only. Either the existence of the same passion or interest in a majority at the same time must be prevented, or the majority, having such coexistent passion or interest, must be rendered, by their number and local situation, unable to concert and carry into effect schemes of oppression. If the impulse and the opportunity be suffered to coincide, we well know that neither moral nor religious motives can be relied on as an adequate control. They are not found to be such on the injustice and violence of individuals, and lose their efficacy in proportion to the number combined together, that is, in proportion as their efficacy becomes needful.

From this view of the subject it may be concluded that a pure democracy, by which I mean a society consisting of a small number of citizens, who assemble and administer the government in person, can admit of no cure for the mischiefs of faction. A common passion or interest will, in almost every case, be felt by a majority

45

of the whole; a communication and concert result from the form of government itself; and there is nothing to check the inducements to sacrifice the weaker party or an obnoxious individual. Hence it is that such democracies have ever been spectacles of turbulence and contention; have ever been found incompatible with personal security or the rights of property; and have in general been as short in their lives as they have been violent in their deaths. Theoretic politicians, who have patronized this species of government, have erroneously supposed that by reducing mankind to a perfect equality in their political rights, they would, at the same time, be perfectly equalized and assimilated in their possessions, their opinions, and their passions.

A republic, by which I mean a government in which the scheme of representation takes place, opens a different prospect, and promises the cure for which we are seeking. Let us examine the points in which it varies from pure democracy, and we shall comprehend both the nature of the cure and the efficacy which it must derive from the Union.

The two great points of difference between a democracy and a republic are: first, the delegation of the government, in the latter, to a small number of citizens elected by the rest; secondly, the greater number of citizens, and greater sphere of country, over which the latter may be extended.

The effect of the first difference is, on the one hand, to refine and enlarge the public views, by passing them through the medium of a chosen body of citizens, whose wisdom may best discern the true interest of their country, and whose patriotism and love of justice will be least likely to sacrifice it to temporary or partial considerations. Under such a regulation, it may well happen that the public voice, pronounced by the representatives of the people, will be more consonant to the public good than if pronounced by the people themselves, convened for the purpose. On the other hand, the effect may be inverted. Men of factious tempers, of local prejudices, or of sinister designs, may, by intrigue,

46

by corruption, or by other means, first obtain the suffrages, and then betray the interests, of the people. The question resulting is, whether small or extensive republics are more favorable to the election of proper guardians of the public weal; and it is clearly decided in favor of the latter by two obvious considerations:

In the first place, it is to be remarked that, however small the republic may be, the representatives must be raised to a certain number, in order to guard against the cabals of a few; and that, however large it may be, they must be limited to a certain number, in order to guard against the confusion of a multitude. Hence, the number of representatives in the two cases not being in proportion to that of the two constituents, and being proportionally greater in the small republic, it follows that, if the proportion of fit characters be not less in the large than in the small republic, the former will present a greater option, and consequently a greater probability of a fit choice.

In the next place, as each representative will be chosen by a greater number of citizens in the large than in the small republic, it will be more difficult for unworthy candidates to practise with success the vicious arts by which elections are too often carried; and the suffrages of the people being more free, will be more likely to centre in men who possess the most attractive merit and the most diffusive and established characters.

It must be confessed that in this, as in most other cases, there is a mean, on both sides of which inconveniences will be found to lie. By enlarging too much the number of electors, you render the representative too little acquainted with all their local circumstances and lesser interests; as by reducing it too much, you render him unduly attached to these, and too little fit to comprehend and pursue great and national objects. The federal Constitution forms a happy combination in this respect; the great and aggregate interests being referred to the national, the local and particular to the State legislatures.

The other point of difference is, the greater number of citi-

47

zens and extent of territory which may be brought within the compass of republican than of democratic government; and it is this circumstance principally which renders factious combinations less to be dreaded in the former than in the latter. The smaller the society, the fewer probably will be the distinct parties and interests composing it; the fewer the distinct parties and interests, the more frequently will a majority be found of the same party; and the smaller the number of individuals composing a majority, and the smaller the compass within which they are placed, the most easily will they concert and execute their plans of oppression. Extend the sphere, and you take in a greater variety of parties and interests; you make it less probable that a majority of the whole will have a common motive to invade the rights of other citizens; or if such a common motive exists, it will be more difficult for all who feel it to discover their own strength, and to act in unison with each other. Besides other impediments, it may be remarked that, where there is a consciousness of unjust or dishonorable purposes, communication is always checked by distrust in proportion to the number whose concurrence is necessary.

Hence, it clearly appears, that the same advantage which a republic has over a democracy, in controlling the effects of faction, is enjoyed by a large over a small republic, -- is enjoyed by the Union over the States composing it. Does the advantage consist in the substitution of representatives whose enlightened views and virtuous sentiments render them superior to local prejudices and to schemes of injustice? It will not be denied that the representation of the Union will be most likely to possess these requisite endowments. Does it consist in the greater security afforded by a greater variety of parties, against the event of any one party being able to outnumber and oppress the rest? In an equal degree does the increased variety of parties comprised within the Union, increase this security. Does it, in fine, consist in the greater obstacles opposed to the concert and accomplishment of the secret wishes of an unjust and interested majority? Here, again, the ex-

48

tent of the Union gives it the most palpable advantage.

The influence of factious leaders may kindle a flame within their particular States, but will be unable to spread a general conflagration through the other States. A religious sect may degenerate into a political faction in a part of the Confederacy; but the variety of sects dispersed over the entire face of it must secure the national councils against any danger from that source. A rage for paper money, for an abolition of debts, for an equal division of property, or for any other improper or wicked project, will be less apt to pervade the whole body of the Union than a particular member of it; in the same proportion as such a malady is more likely to taint a particular county or district, than an entire State.

In the extent and proper structure of the Union, therefore, we behold a republican remedy for the diseases most incident to republican government. And according to the degree of pleasure and pride we feel in being republicans, ought to be our zeal in cherishing the spirit and supporting the character of Federalists.

PUBLIUS

MADISON

One of the strongest arguments in support of the proposed Constitution is that it establishes a government capable of controlling
the violence and damage caused by factions. Factions are groups
of people who combine together to protect and promote their special economic interests and political opinions. These factions
are often at odds with each other, frequently work against the
public interest, and infringe upon the rights of others.

Both supporters and opponents of democratic government are
concerned with the political instability produced by rival factions
competing for power. Our state governments have not succeeded in
solving this problem; in fact, the situation is so acute that many
people are disillusioned with all politicians and blame government, in general, for all their problems. Consequently, a form of
popular government that can deal successfully with this problem
has a great deal to recommend it.

Given the nature of man, factions are inevitable. As long
as men hold different opinions and are unequal in wealth and the
amount of property they own, they will continue to associate with
those who are similar to them. There are many reasons, serious
and trivial, which account for the formation of factions, but the
most important and durable source of faction is the unequal distribution of property. Men of greater ability and talent tend to
possess more property than those of lesser ability, and since the
first object of government is to protect and encourage ability,
it follows that the rights of property owners must be protected.
Property is divided unequally and, in addition, there are many
different kinds of property; men have different interests depending upon the kind of property they own. For example, the interests of landowners differ from those who own businesses. Govern-

ment must not only protect the conflicting interests of property owners, it must, at the same time, successfully regulate the conflicts that result from those who own, and those who do not own, property.

Governmental regulation of factions is a difficult task. Legislators are human, and the laws they pass often reflect their own self-interests or the narrow interests of a few factions. The apportionment of taxes, for example, should demand the strictest impartiality, but legislators, more often than not, think first of their own pocketbooks.

If factions are both inevitable and troublesome, how are we to deal with them? There are two alternatives: the first is to remove the causes of faction; the second alternative is to establish a government capable of controlling the effects of factions. Let us see why the second alternative is preferable and how it will work if the Constitution is adopted.

We say factions are inevitable. But we are speaking here of democratic societies where men can openly disagree and are free to form groups to protect their interests. Totalitarian or tyrannical governments do not allow factions to develop in the first place. Men may differ or disagree in totalitarian nations, but they are forced to remain silent. If we choose to rid ourselves of factions by taking away liberty, it could be truly said that our "cure is worse than the disease." The only other way to prevent the formation of factions is to make certain that men are all alike in their beliefs, opinions, passions, abilities, and interests. But to work for this, or wish for such a situation, is quite obviously unrealistic, if not absurd.

Some people claim that enlightened political leaders (regardless of the form of government) can effectively arbitrate or reconcile clashing factious interests, but men in public office will not always be fair and wise. They will frequently put immediate and selfish interests ahead of the future good of the country.

We must conclude that the causes of faction either cannot, or

51

should not, be removed. Instead, we must look to the means of controlling the damage factions create. The government established by the Constitution does just this.

The framers established a <u>representative</u> form of government. A representative form of government is one in which the many elect the few who govern. Pure or direct democracies (countries in which all the citizens participate directly in making the laws) cannot possibly control factious conflicts. This is because the strongest and largest faction dominates, and there is no way to protect weak factions against the actions of an obnoxious individual or a strong majority. Direct democracies cannot effectively protect personal and property rights and have always been characterized by conflict.

If the new plan of government is adopted, we <u>hope</u> that the men elected to office will be wise and good men--the best America has to offer. Theoretically, those who govern should be the least likely to sacrifice the public good to temporary or petty considerations, <u>but</u> we must be aware that the very opposite might happen. Men who are members of particular factions, or who have prejudices or evil motives might manage, by intrigue or corruption, to win elections and <u>then</u> betray the interests of the people. However, the possibility of this happening in a large country, such as ours, is greatly reduced. The likelihood that public office will be held by qualified men is greater in large countries because there will be more representatives chosen by a greater number of citizens. This makes it more difficult for the candidates to deceive the people. Representative government is needed in large countries, not to protect the people from the tyranny of the few, but to guard against the rule of the mob.

In large republics factions will be numerous, but they will be weaker than in small, direct democracies where it is easier for factions to consolidate their strength. In this country leaders of factions may be able to influence state governments to support unsound economic and political policies--to promote, for example,

52

an equal division of property--but their influence will not extend to the national government.

We can conclude by saying that the problems presented by the <u>structure</u> of representative government can be solved by the application of republican <u>principles</u>.

A strong national government is essential to the defense of the
nation, to harmonious relationships among the states, and to the
effective regulation of commerce. Unless the national government
is strengthened, the United States, like many European countries,
may fall under the control of a small military group or become
disastrously torn by faction. These are all compelling reasons to
adopt the Constitution, but we still hear the argument that America is too large for a republican form of government.

There is considerable confusion on this issue. In a previous
Paper we established that the republican form is suited to a large
country; the fact that the objection still survives suggests that
the opponents of the Constitution confuse a republic with a democracy. In a democracy, all the people meet together, formulate
policies, and pass laws; in a republic, policies are formulated
and laws are passed by representatives elected or selected by the
people. This distinction ought to make it clear that it is a democracy, not a republic, that cannot operate successfully in a large
country.

This error in terminology explains the confusion in large
part. It can be traced to some well-known European writers who
lived in monarchies. These writers defend that form of government
(monarchies) by pointing to the problems that existed in ancient
democracies and modern republics. Readers of their work assume
that the authors use the terms "republic" and "democracy" synony-
mously.

The government proposed in the Constitution is both republican and federal in form. A federal form of government is one in
which power is divided between the states and the central government. In addition, the national government consists of powers

54

specifically delegated to it; the states, far from being abolished, retain much of their sovereignty. If the framers had abolished the state governments, the opponents of the proposed government would have a legitimate objection to it.

The immediate object of the Constitution is to bring the present thirteen states into a secure union, but no doubt new states will be added. Almost every state, old and new, will have one boundary next to territory owned by a foreign nation. The states farthest from the center of the country will be most endangered by these foreign countries; they may find it inconvenient to send representatives long distances to the capitol, but in terms of safety and protection they stand to gain the most from a strong national government.

I present these arguments confident that you will not listen to those "prophets of gloom" who say that the proposed government is unworkable. It seems incredible to me that these gloomy voices suggest we abandon the idea of combining together in strength--we have fought a war together; our interests are common interests. Are we so afraid of innovation, of novelty, so timid and set in our ways that we will allow our hard-won liberties to come to nothing? Surely your good sense and understanding of our past experiences combine to give you confidence that a representative form of government best protects private rights and the public welfare. There was no precedent for the Revolution; we cannot afford to wait for precedent now. The war was boldly undertaken and though the government of the Confederacy was unique when it was devised, it was meant to be improved as circumstances change.

HAMILTON

Many weaknesses and problems of the existing government have been discussed, but there are a few others which merit our attention.

Problem number 1: Both Federalists and anti-Federalists agree that the lack of power to regulate commerce among the several states and between this government and foreign nations has resulted in a deplorable situation. Foreign governments are understandably reluctant to enter into trade agreements or treaties with us knowing that the individual states can (and do) violate, at their whim, the terms of these agreements. The United States will never be able to develop a favorable balance of trade or enjoy satisfactory diplomatic relationships under these circumstances. In addition, the lack of uniform trade regulation has resulted in considerable animosity among the states. It is of the utmost importance that the national government have the power to regulate commerce.

Problem number 2: The national defense depends upon a Constitutional grant of power to the national government to raise armies. The revolution exposed the problems of relying upon a state quota system. Several states, in an effort to meet their quotas, promised their male citizens more money than certain other states were paying. Many men, in an attempt to force their states to increase military pay, delayed enlisting. This competition among the states (a form of blackmail, actually) resulted in confusion, great expense, inefficiency, and undisciplined troops. The situation was so serious that only the enthusiasm for liberty on the part of some men kept the army together. In addition, this system of recruitment is unfair. The states nearest the center of the war made the largest effort to meet their quotas; those farthest away from the fighting made little or no effort to meet them.

A state quota system, whether applied to men or money, always results in inefficiency and injustice.

Problem number 3: Under the present system of government, all the states, whether large or small, are equally represented in the Congress. This means that the people are unequally represented. For example, New Hampshire, Rhode Island, New Jersey, Delaware, Georgia, South Carolina, and Maryland constitute a majority of the states, but they do not contain one-third of the population. This situation violates the republican principles of majority rule. The citizens of the small states must realize that, sooner or later, the citizens of the large states will protest such an unfair arrangement. When that happens, the stability and welfare of the country will be threatened. A situation in which a responsible majority is frequently coerced by a small minority could result in anarchy.

A national government controlled by a legislative minority is particularly vulnerable to foreign influence and corruption. It is difficult for a foreign government to influence a governing majority but relatively easy for them to corrupt or influence a powerful few. It is interesting that monarchies are in a better position to thwart manipulation by foreign governments. Kings, true enough, have no scruples about sacrificing the welfare of their subjects to satisfy their own ambitions, but kings identify so closely with the glory and reputation of the countries they rule that they are not often tempted to give in to the interests of foreign nations.

Problem number 4: The greatest defect of the present government is the lack of a Supreme Court with power to define and interpret the laws. A law means nothing if there is no high court to interpret it. In addition, a Supreme Court is needed to interpret and enforce the terms of treaties. At present, treaties can be ignored or violated by thirteen separate state legislatures and courts. How can foreign governments respect or confide in the United States?

All nations have found it necessary to establish one court with more authority and power than other courts possess. Such a court is especially important in this country where state and national laws can (and often do) conflict. The whole must be greater than its parts. We cannot have good government if local biases and narrow interests are allowed to dominate; men elected to national office cannot escape being influenced by the states to whom, in large part, they owe their public office. Can Americans continue to trust and respect such an unstable government--one in which there is no final arbiter when disputes arise?

Problem number 5: The existing government was ratified by the state legislatures. We feel that ratification of the Constitution ought to come from the people. The state legislatures, by an act of repeal, could do away with the national government altogether! The proposed Constitution calls for special ratifying conventions to be held in each state. Consequently, if the new government is adopted, it will rest upon that great republican principle, the consent of the governed.

This is only a brief review of the most serious defects in the present system. There are others. By this time it ought to be clear to reasonable people that we need an entirely new governmental system. For example, the organization of the Congress is totally inadequate but, unfortunately, we cannot correct all the weaknesses of the governmental system by simply reorganizing the Legislative branch. We need an Executive and Judicial branch; we need a new legislative structure--two houses instead of one--a Senate and a House of Representatives. If this Constitution is not ratified, the government will still have to be strengthened somehow. There is every reason to assume that additional power would be granted to the Congress. The result would be one branch of government called upon to do the job of three. What a political monstrosity! The very tyranny the opponents of the Constitution are so eager to avoid would be the result.

HAMILTON

Americans agree that the national government ought to be in charge
of the nation's military forces in time of war, but some people
feel that the Constitution should prohibit the existence of standing armies in peacetime. This argument is vague and illogical.
A stranger in our country, reading our newspapers, would conclude
that the Constitution either demands that armies be maintained during peacetime, or that the president has the sole power of raising
troops and waging war.

If this stranger, however, studied the Constitution, he would
realize immediately that the power to raise armies is granted to
the Congress, not the president, and that even the Congress is
limited in its power to maintain a military establishment. The
Constitution states clearly that Congress may not appropriate
money for the support of an army for more than two years. This
should reduce the fears of those people who think that an army will
be maintained without the necessity for it.

This stranger, however, might still be baffled; he would quite
naturally think, in view of all the objection, that there must be
some reason for this strong sentiment. He might conclude that the
state constitutions and the Articles of Confederation prohibit the
raising of armies during peace. But that is not the case; the
constitutions of Pennsylvania and North Carolina suggest that
peacetime military establishments might threaten liberty. The
other eleven state constitutions either allow peacetime armies or
are silent on the matter and, surprisingly, the Articles of Confederation restrict the power of the states in this regard, but
not the national government. Knowing these facts, what can such a
stranger conclude except that the opponents of the Constitution
are deliberately trying to excite the people?

But instead of worrying about the arguments against maintaining a military establishment during peacetime, we will examine the merits of doing so. It is true that an ocean separates us from Europe, but we are surrounded by territories belonging to foreign nations. Furthermore, the savage Indian tribes on our western frontier have more to gain by being friendly to these European powers than to us. Improvements in navigation will result in closer political ties between Britain and Spain. As we become stronger it is certain that these two great maritime powers will increase their military establishments in our country. For this reason we will have to increase the size of our military posts, not only to protect ourselves but to make trade with the Indians possible. It is impractical and unwise to draw men from the state militia to man these posts during peacetime. Men will not want to leave their jobs and families for short periods of duty; the wisest and most practical plan is to maintain a permanent corps in the pay of the United States government.

Also, we must look to the future. If we hope to be secure on this continent and to increase trade with foreign nations, we ought to have a navy. While we are building our naval strength we will need garrisons to protect the dockyards and arsenals.

HAMILTON

Some people are saying that the proposed government will not be
able to operate or enforce the laws without the aid of a military
force. This argument, like so many advanced by opponents of the
Constitution, is weak and vague. These opponents seem to feel
that the people will object to any exercise of national authority
in the internal affairs of the states. They do not, incidentally,
make a clear distinction between internal and external affairs.
In addition, they assume that the national government will not be
administered as well as the state governments are.

I think the very opposite will be true; the national government is set up in such a way that it will be better administered
than the state governments are at present. The Congress will be
composed, in part, of representatives elected by the people, thereby giving them greater power in the affairs of government, and the
Senate promises to be a particularly distinguished group since its
members will be screened and selected by the state legislatures.
The Senate will not be torn by local faction or partisan interests
and, being far from the scene of local politics, will not give in
to schemes against the public good. (More of this when we examine
the Senate in greater detail.) There is simply nothing to suggest
that the national government will not be administered well, or that
it will need force to execute the laws.

The hope of not being punished for insurrection encourages it;
the dread of punishment, on the other hand, discourages it. Is it
not more likely that the national government, possessing sufficient
power and able to call on the resources of the states, will be in
a better position than the states alone to keep the peace and deal
with faction? A faction may be able to cause trouble within a
state, may even win over the state's political leaders, but such a

faction would be no match for the national government.

I have a theory (which you may be tempted to reject simply because it is new) that as the national government becomes familiar to the people, as it begins to affect them in their daily lives, their respect and attachment to it will increase. "Man is very much a creature of habit." If the national government stays out of sight, it will stay out of mind, but if it reaches into the internal affairs of the states, the people will feel comfortable with it, and there will be less occasion or necessity for the government to use force.

Under the proposed plan of government all citizens will be under the authority of both the national and state governments. After awhile, the distinction between state and national authority will become blurred. The national government will have no more trouble than the states in securing obedience to its laws and, in addition, the prestige of the national government will be enhanced because it can call on the combined resources of all the states. Under the proposed government, the Constitution and the national laws will become the SUPREME LAW of the land; all state officials will have to take an oath to uphold them. Consequently, the state legislatures, the state courts, and the governors will be a part of the national government--but only so far "as its just and constitutional authority extends." This point is emphasized to answer those who fear the Constitution abolishes the state governments.

If these points are properly considered there should be every expectation that the national laws will be peacefully and effectively executed. You may assume the opposite if you wish, for there is no guarantee under any form of government that power will not be abused. But I still must ask the opponents of the Constitution what ambitious and evil men would gain by ignoring the public good or the obligations of duty.

62

HAMILTON

To the People of the State of New ·York:

In disquisitions of every kind, there are certain primary truths, or first principles, upon which all subsequent reasonings must depend. These contain an internal evidence which, antecedent to all reflection or combination, commands the assent of the mind. Where it produces not this effect, it must proceed either from some defect or disorder in the organs of perception, or from the influence of some strong interest, or passion, or prejudice. Of this nature are the maxims in geometry, that "the whole is greater than its parts; things equal to the same are equal to one another; two straight lines cannot enclose a space; and all right angles are equal to each other." Of the same nature are these other maxims in ethics and politics, that there cannot be an effect without a cause; that the means ought to be proportioned to the end; that every power ought to be commensurate with its object; that there ought to be no limitation of a power destined to effect a purpose which is itself incapable of limitation. And there are other truths in the two latter sciences which, if they cannot pretend to rank in the class of axioms, are yet such direct inferences from them, and so obvious in themselves, and so agreeable to the natural and unsophisticated dictates of common-sense, that they challenge the assent of a sound and unbiased mind, with a degree of force and conviction almost equally irresistible.

The objects of geometrical inquiry are so entirely abstracted from those pursuits which stir up and put in motion the unruly passions of the human heart, that mankind, without difficulty, adopt not only the more simple theorems of the science, but even those abstruse paradoxes which, however they may appear susceptible of demonstration, are at variance with the natural conceptions which the mind, without the aid of philosophy, would be led to entertain upon the subject. The infinite divisibility of matter, or, in other words, the infinite divisibility of a finite thing, extending even to the minutest atom, is a point agreed among geometricians, though not less incomprehensible to common-sense than any of those mysteries in religion, against which the batteries of infidelity have been so industriously levelled.

But in the sciences of morals and politics, men are found far less tractable. To a certain degree, it is right and useful that this should be the case. Caution and investigation are a necessary armor against error and imposition. But this untractableness may be carried too far, and may degenerate into obstinacy, perverseness, or disingenuity. Though it cannot be pretended that the principles of moral and political knowledge have, in general, the same degree of certainty with those of the mathematics, yet they have much better claims in this respect tnan, to judge from the conduct of men in particular situations, we should be disposed to allow them. The obscurity is much oftener in the passions and prejudices of the reasoner than in the subject. Men, upon too many occasions, do not give their own understandings fair play; but, yielding to some untoward bias, they entangle themselves in words and confound themselves in subtleties.

How else could it happen (if we admit the objectors to be sincere in their opposition), that positions so clear as those which manifest the necessity of a general power of taxation in the government of the Union, should have to encounter any adversaries among men of discernment? Though these positions have been elsewhere fully stated, they will perhaps not be improperly recapitulated in this place, as introductory to an examination of what may have been offered by way of objection to them. They are in substance as follows:

A government ought to contain in itself every power requisite to the full accomplishment of the objects committed to its care,

and to the complete execution of the trusts for which it is responsible, free from every other control but a regard to the public
good and to the sense of the people.

As the duties of superintending the national defence and of
securing the public peace against foreign or domestic violence involve a provision for casualties and dangers to which no possible
limits can be assigned, the power of making that provision ought
to know no other bounds that the exigencies of the nation and the
resources of the community.

As revenue is the essential engine by which the means of an-
swering the national exigencies must be procured, the power of procuring that article in its full extent must necessarily be comprehended in that of providing for those exigencies.

As theory and practice conspire to prove that the power of
procuring revenue is unavailing when exercised over the States in
their collective capacities, the federal government must of necessity be invested with an unqualified power of taxation in the ordinary modes.

Did not experience evince the contrary, it would be natural
to conclude that the propriety of a general power of taxation in
the national government might safely be permitted to rest on the
evidence of these propositions, unassisted by any additional arguments or illustrations. But we find, in fact, that the antagonists
of the proposed Constitution, so far from acquiescing in their
justness or truth, seem to make their principal and most zealous
effort against this part of the plan. It may therefore be satisfactory to analyze the arguments with which they combat it.

Those of them which have been most labored with that view,
seem in substance to amount to this: "It is not true, because the
exigencies of the Union may not be susceptible of limitation, that
its power of laying taxes ought to be unconfined. Revenue is as
requisite to the purposes of the local administrations as to those
of the Union; and the former are at least of equal importance with
the latter to the happiness of the people. It is, therefore, as

65

necessary that the State governments should be able to command the means of supplying their wants, as that the national government should possess the like faculty in respect to the wants of the Union. But an indefinite power of taxation in the *latter* might, and probably would in time, deprive the *former* of the means of providing for their own necessities; and would subject them entirely to the mercy of the national legislature. As the laws of the Union are to become the supreme law of the land, as it is to have power to pass all laws that may be necessary for carrying into execution the authorities with which it is proposed to vest it, the national government might at any time abolish the taxes imposed for State objects upon the pretence of an interference with its own. It might allege a necessity of doing this in order to give efficacy to the national revenues. And thus all the resources of taxation might by degrees become the subjects of federal monopoly, to the entire exclusion and destruction of the State government."

This mode of reasoning appears sometimes to turn upon the supposition of usurpation in the national government; at other times it seems to be designed only as a deduction from the constitutional operation of its intended powers. It is only in the latter light that it can be admitted to have any pretensions to fairness. The moment we launch into conjectures about the usurpations of the federal government, we get into an unfathomable abyss, and fairly put ourselves out of the reach of all reasoning. Imagination may range at pleasure till it gets bewildered amidst the labyrinths of an enchanged castle, and knows not on which side to turn to extricate itself from the perplexities into which it so rashly has adventured. Whatever may be the limits or modifications of the powers of the Union, it is easy to imagine an endless train of possible dangers; and by indulging an excess of jealousy and timidity, we may bring ourselves to a state of absolute scepticism and irresolution. I repeat here what I have observed in substance in another place, that all observations founded upon the danger of usurpation ought to be referred to the composition and structure of the government, not to the nature or extent of its powers. The State governments, by their original constitutions, are invested with complete sovereignty. In what does our security consist against usurpation from that quarter? Doubtless in the manner of their formation, and in a due dependence of those who are to administer them upon the people. If the proposed construction of the federal government be found, upon an impartial examination of it, to be such as to afford, to a proper extent, the same species of security, all apprehensions on the score of usurpation ought to be discarded.

It should not be forgotten that a disposition in the State governments to encroach upon the rights of the Union is quite as probable as a disposition in the Union to encroach upon the rights of the State governments. What side would be likely to prevail in such a conflict, must depend on the means which the contending parties could employ towards insuring success. As in republics strength is always on the side of the people, and as there are weighty reasons to induce a belief that the State governments will commonly possess most influence over them, the natural conclusion is that such contests will be most apt to end to the disadvantage of the Union; and that there is greater probability of encroachments by the members upon the federal head, than by the federal head upon the members. But it is evident that all conjectures of this kind must be extremely vague and fallible: and that it is by far the safest course to lay them altogether aside, and to confine our attention wholly to the nature and extent of the powers as they are delineated in the Constitution. Every thing beyond this must be left to the prudence and firmness of the people; who, as they will hold the scales in their own hands, it is to be hoped, will always take care to preserve the constitutional equilibrium between the general and the State governments. Upon this ground, which is evidently the true one, it will not be difficult to obviate the objections which have been made to an indefinite power of taxation in the United States.   PUBLIUS

67

31

HAMILTON

In the discussion of politics, like any other matter, certain
truths or first principles must be understood and accepted. First
principles are more easily accepted in mathematics and science than
in politics. For example, a first principle in geometry is that
the whole is greater than its parts; another, that two straight
lines cannot enclose a space. These abstract principles are not
disturbing or controversial. But the moment we turn from science
and mathematics to political and moral issues, acceptance of first
principles becomes very difficult. This is understandable; after
all, politics and morals directly influence our lives, and the
principles involved are less exact than those in mathematics or
science. Nevertheless, first principles do operate in politics,
and it is important to put aside subjective judgments in order to
examine them.

An important first principle in politics is that the central
(or national) government ought to possess a general and broad power
of taxation. This power to tax should be limited only by the nation's needs and the national resources available. How can the
national government promote the general welfare, provide for the
national defense, or carry out any of its many other duties if it
has not the revenue to do these things? All the powers granted to
the national government come to nothing if it has no (or limited)
power to raise money. This should be obvious, but opponents of
the proposed government are particularly critical of the taxing
power provided for in the Constitution. What is the nature of
their argument?

The opponents claim that even though the needs of the country
cannot be limited by defining them, the taxing power of the national government should be limited. They point out that the states,

as well as the national government, need revenue and have the right to tax their citizens. They argue that because the national government under the Constitution is superior to the state governments, it is conceivable that some day the national government will deprive the states of their right to tax.

If this argument reflects a general fear of a strong national government, there is no logical way to answer it. No matter what limits are placed on the powers of the national government, some people will object--they will say that the national government is still too powerful. I can only repeat what I have said before; those who fear that too much power is vested in the national government should, once again, examine the structure of the government (division of power between the states and the national government and the three branches of the national government with their checks and balances), rather than worry about the nature and extent of power granted to either governmental unit. The federal structure of the government will prevent the national government from gaining too much power.

It is just as likely that the states will encroach upon the rights and powers of the national government, as the other way around. In a republic, such as ours, the people are the ultimate source of power, and the state governments will have more influence over them than the national government will have. Therefore, in a conflict between the national and state governments, the latter are apt to have the advantage. But all this is speculative. We have every reason to hope that the people will guard the constitutional balance between the national and state governments.

69

37

MADISON

We reviewed the defects of the existing government in order to convince you that a new government must be at least as energetic and strong as the one proposed. But in urging ratification we do not expect you to accept the merits of the Constitution on faith alone. We will examine all the provisions of the Constitution, compare each provision with the others, and will attempt to calculate the effects of the new government on the nation and its citizens.

It is one of the ironies of human affairs that important public matters are seldom examined objectively. It is small wonder, then, that a new plan of government excites passions and prejudices. It seems evident to us, based upon what they have written, that those who oppose the Constitution have only scanned it. These opponents hope, no doubt, to keep their prejudices intact. Frequently, those who write in favor of the Constitution are just as guilty of bias; much of what we read on both sides of the issue lacks substance and critical analysis. However, there is a difference between those biased in favor of the Constitution and those who are biased against it. Many people who support the Constitution, though they are ill informed about it, do so because they know the existing government is weak and our situation is serious. We can forgive them their quick and uncritical enthusiasm. The biased opponent, on the other hand, can have no praiseworthy motive at all.

This Paper is not addressed to either of the two biased groups. It is written for those of you who sincerely want to promote the welfare of the country and who are open to reasonable arguments and explanations. To appreciate the virtues of the proposed government, you must realize that no plan is faultless. The Convention, like all groups, was composed of fallible men; fallible men drafted the

Constitution, and fallible men will judge it.

We must not only accept the fallibility of men; we must try to understand what a difficult task the framers faced. What was done in Philadelphia has never been done before. The framers began their deliberations knowing that the structure of the existing government is weak because the underlying principles of that government are unsound. They could not erect a strong structure upon a weak foundation. Where did they find the principles upon which to build? The framers could not look to other confederacies because they, too, were founded on unsound principles. Studying both ancient and modern confederacies served only to warn them of what should be avoided in the establishment of the new government. As a result, the framers took as their "textbook" the experience, rather than the theories, of this and other countries.

One of the most important and difficult problems was how to establish an energetic and stable government without threatening the liberties of the people. Had the framers not solved this problem, they would have failed the object of the Convention and the expectation of the people. Stability in government promotes confidence and is essential to national character. Stability is threatened if too many people hold power, and energetic government requires that the execution of the laws should be the responsibility of one man, the president. But in a free society power is derived from the people and those who hold office are responsible to them. The proposed government reconciles and balances these two important values. Stability is achieved through the principle of representation; liberty is protected because the government rests upon the consent of the people. In addition, a part of this balance was achieved by establishing relatively short terms of office for representatives, senators, and the president.

Another problem the framers faced was how best to divide authority and power between the state and national governments. Every reflective person knows how difficult it is to separate the various spheres of the natural world. The mind is an excellent

71

example. Who can divide sense, perception, judgment, desire, memory, and imagination? Naturalists have great difficulty separating organic from inorganic matter and distinguishing between vegetable and animal life. We know these divisions in the natural world are perfect; it is only man who cannot accurately discern them. Consider, then, the near impossibility of determining proper divisions of function and power in man-made institutions.

The framers also had to wrestle with the problem of describing in specific detail the purpose and limits of different codes of laws and types of courts. The English studied this problem for years, and there is still no precise division between common law and statute law, or between maritime, ecclesiastical, and corporate law; the jurisdiction of many English courts is unclear. All new laws, no matter how carefully written, remain somewhat vague until they are broken and the court interprets their meaning. The complexity of these matters presents trouble enough, but there is still a further problem: we perceive ideas differently--we not only perceive ideas differently; we express these ideas in words and, unfortunately, no language supplies words and phrases for every complex idea or is so precise that every word has only one meaning.

The Convention faced other problems. The delegates had to reconcile the conflict and competition between the large and small states. It was only natural that the large and influential states would contend for greater power in the new government and equally natural that the small states would be reluctant to relinquish the power they now have under the Articles of Confederation. It was unrealistic to hope for anything other than compromise to end this conflict. Even after the compromise was worked out (equal representation in the Senate and proportional representation in the House), the larger states tried to gain greater power in the House, where they had an advantage, and the small states worked equally hard to increase the power of the Senate where they had the most to gain. It is undeniable that the Constitution reflects this struggle.

There were other conflicts: competing sectional interests had to be reconciled as did various economic and social conflicts within each state. These competing interests will undoubtedly have a beneficial effect on the proposed government (discussed in another Paper), but to reconcile them during the Convention was a difficult task.

It is remarkable, considering all these pressures and difficulties, that agreement was reached on the fundamental structure of the government; after all, it is easy for a theorist to plan a perfect document in the privacy of his den or imagination, but for men to hammer out their differences together is another matter. We took note (in a previous Paper) of the repeated, but unsuccessful, attempts made in the United Netherlands to reform the worst features of their constitution.

Two reasons help to account for the success of our Constitutional Convention: (1) the framers were free of party animosities (the most common failing of deliberative groups), and (2) the delegates were so pleased with the final product that they were willing to put aside certain personal objections in order to avoid further delay or the necessity of drafting an entirely new document.

MADISON

The purpose of this Paper is to determine whether or not the framers established a republican form of government. No other form is suited to the particular genius of the American people; only a republican form of government can carry forward the principles fought for in the Revolution or demonstrate that self-government is both possible and practical.

What, then, are the distinctive characteristics of the republican form? Unfortunately, we cannot find the answer by reading certain books which purport to describe the constitutions of republican nations. For example, Holland, Venice, and Poland are described by political writers as republics, but the power in all three governments is not derived from the people; it is held by kings, nobles, or a small group of people. Since the term "republic" is loosely used, we must look to the theoretical principles of republicanism as they have been defined.

A republican form of government is one which derives its powers either directly or indirectly from the people and is administered by persons who hold public office for a limited period of time or during good behavior. No government can be called republican that derives its power from a few people or from a favored and wealthy class. Appointment to public office (as opposed to election) does not violate the principles of republicanism as long as the government rests upon the consent of the governed.

The Constitution conforms to these republican principles. The House of Representatives is directly elected by the people; the senators and the president are indirectly selected by them. Even the judges will reflect the choice of the people since the president appoints them, and their appointment is confirmed by the Senate. The president, senators, and representatives hold office for a specified and limited term; judges are appointed for life--subject, however, to good behavior. The constitutional prohibition against granting titles of nobility and the guarantee to the states that they shall enjoy a republican form of government is further proof that the new government is republican in nature.

These facts, however, do not satisfy some people. We hear that the Convention destroyed the federal aspect of the government by taking away too much power from the states. According to these opponents, the framers established a national form of government--one in which the citizens are acted upon directly (as citizens of the nation instead of citizens of the states). Actually, the proposed government contains both national and federal characteristics. It is true that the national government will have authority over individuals as national citizens, but in many important respects the new plan of government is clearly federal in its form. The principle of federalism (division of power between the states and the national government) is reflected in the suggested method of ratification. The delegates to the ratifying conventions will vote as citizens of their states, not as citizens of the nation. The federal form is also reflected in the structure of the Senate in which the states are equally represented. The fact that the states retain certain exclusive and important powers is further proof of the federal nature of the proposed government. But we are not going to claim that there are no national features. Of course there are. We can conclude by saying that in its structure, the new government is both national and federal; in the operation of its powers, it is national; in the extent of its powers, it is federal.

MADISON

Some people contend that the framers exceeded their authority by drafting a new form of government. How can we answer this charge?

We answer by saying: the purpose of the Convention could not be achieved by the method the framers were instructed to use. The purpose of the Convention was to strengthen the national government in order to save the Union; in order to accomplish this, the delegates were empowered to alter or add to the provisions in the Articles of Confederation. However, it quickly became apparent that neither alterations or new provisions could transform the Articles into an adequate system of government. The framers had to decide whether to preserve a weak government or establish a strong one. In deciding the way they did, they chose the end over the means, the purpose over the method.

Actually, the framers did not scrap the Articles of Confederation altogether. Many principles of the old government remain in the new one. For example, the states retain much of their power and, in some cases, the new government will continue to exercise its power over the states as political entities rather than over individuals directly. It can be argued that the framers built the new government upon the fundamental principles of the old one.

The Convention did exceed the powers granted to it in the matter of ratification. They were commissioned to strengthen the existing government and, then, to submit their revised plan to Congress. Congress, in turn, was to submit the Constitution to the state legislatures for ratification. But the framers have reported out a Constitution which they recommend be considered for adoption by delegates elected to special ratifying conventions in each state. They further recommend that the Constitution should go into effect after ratification in nine states only. It is interesting that this bold change in the rules is the least criticized feature of the Constitution; perhaps people realize the unfairness of subjecting the fate of the entire nation to the actions of one state.

We examine the Constitution as though it has already been adopted. I think it has withstood that analysis, but we must remember that, at present, it is nothing more than a plan; it has no force whatever until the people approve it. This realization should enable us to judge fairly and calmly what took place in Philadelphia.

The men who drafted the Constitution were deeply aware of the governmental crisis facing the country; they also knew what the people expected of them. They were sobered by their responsibilities, but felt confident that the people were ready for bold decisions. They must have known that too much caution would have betrayed that precious right set forth in the Declaration of Independence--the right of the people to "abolish or alter their government..."

What opponent, no matter how extreme, will not recognize the tacit support given to the framers? After all, twelve of the thirteen states sent delegates to Philadelphia; Congress recommended that the Convention be held; New York, in particular, urged that a Constitutional Convention be convened. But despite all this, for the sake of argument, we will grant that the situation did not justify a new Constitution and those who oppose it did not authorize a new government. Are these sufficient reasons to reject it? There is an old saying that it is "lawful to accept good advice even from an enemy." If this is true, certainly we should accept good advice from friends!

The conclusion is that the Convention did not exceed its power (with the exception of the method to ratify). But even if the framers had exceeded both their power and their obligations, the Constitution they present to us is in the best interests of the nation and ought to be adopted.

MADISON

The preceding Papers reviewed the general form and powers of the
proposed government. I would now like to examine a specific principle of republican government known as the "separation of powers."

One of the principal objections to the Constitution is that
it violates this important principle. The anti-Federalists claim
that the three branches of government are not sufficiently separate and independent and that power is too unevenly distributed.
It is feared that the new government will collapse, and that liberty will be threatened.

I completely agree with those who place great importance on
the separation of powers doctrine and concur with them that a lop-
sided division of power could result in the loss of liberty. If
too much power is granted to any one branch, it does not matter
how many men govern or how they obtain office. Too much (or all)
power in one branch of government is the "very definition of tyranny." If it were true that the Constitution allows such an accu-
mulation of power to develop, no other arguments are needed to
oppose it. I am convinced, however, that this charge cannot be
supported. The question is: how separate should each branch of
government be?

Montesquieu, the French political writer, formulated this
principle of government. He took the British constitution as his
model--which he called, incidentally, "the mirror of political
liberty." Yet the most casual glance at that constitution reveals
that the branches of the British government are far from totally
separate or distinct. For example, the English king acts in a
legislative capacity when he enters into treaties with foreign
sovereigns, because once treaties are signed they have the force
of legislative acts. The English king not only appoints and re-

78

moves judges; he frequently consults them. The judicial branch, then, acts in an advisory capacity to the executive branch. The legislative branch advises the king on constitutional matters and, in cases of impeachment, the House of Lords assumes judicial power. In addition, the judges have such a close relationship with Parliament that they often participate in its deliberations and debates. From these few facts alone, we can infer that Montesquieu, when he wrote that "there can be no liberty where the legislative and executive powers are united in the same person...or, if the power of judging be not separated from the legislative and executive powers," did not mean that the powers should remain absolutely separate or that each branch should not have any control over the other branches.

If we look at the state constitutions we find that there is no state in which the branches of government are absolutely separate and distinct. New Hampshire, whose state constitution is the most recent, seems to have been most fully aware of the impossibility of total separation among the branches. The constitution of this state is less specific on the subject than other state constitutions, yet a careful reading of it makes clear that it was drafted with the separation principle in mind. It also allows for the overlap of powers.

The state constitutions do not violate the separation of powers doctrine set forth by Montesquieu, and neither does the United States Constitution you are now being asked to consider.

WHY THE BRANCHES SHOULD NOT BE COMPLETELY SEPARATE

MADISON

In the last Paper we discussed some of the issues raised by the doctrine known as the "separation of powers." This principle of republican government does not imply that the three branches ought to be completely separate and independent. The very opposite is true. In order that this doctrine can operate effectively, each branch of government must have sufficient power to impose some restraints over the other two.

The Constitution grants to each branch certain exclusive powers. These powers should not be interfered with. However, power not carefully controlled tends to expand. Our first task is to understand and distinguish the differences between legislative, executive, and judicial power. This is necessary to protect the legitimate powers of each branch.

It is not enough to simply set forth on paper what the proper boundaries are. There must be some latitude--some overlap--in the definition of powers assigned to each branch. Experience with our state governments has shown that theoretical checks written into the state constitutions are inadequate, particularly in preventing the growth of legislative power. The most serious mistake made by the framers of republican forms of government is that they concerned themselves exclusively with the problem of too much executive power. They forgot that legislative tyranny is as evil as executive tyranny.

In hereditary monarchies the king is feared; in direct democracies the executive is also feared because the legislative branch is too large to effectively check the executive, and power is so highly diffused that conflicts are difficult to resolve. In direct democracies, the legislature cannot tyrannize because it cannot govern.

In the proposed government, however, it is the legislative branch that is most likely to abuse power. More power, both unde-fined and unlimited, has been granted to it than to the other two branches. In addition, the legislative branch controls the money and has the greatest influence in the determination of salaries paid to government employees. Such a situation invites corruption. Presidential power, on the other hand, is simpler in nature, and the Constitution clearly defines and limits it. The same is true of judicial power. Any attempt by these two branches to infringe upon the Congress would be quickly detected and blocked.

MADISON

After Jefferson finished writing "Notes on the State of Virginia," he added a rough draft of a constitution he hoped would be adopted at a state constitutional convention held in 1783. This draft constitution, like everything Jefferson wrote, is original and comprehensive. It is especially pertinent now, because Jefferson draws our attention to the weaknesses, as well as to the strengths, of a republican form of government. One of his proposals, intended to prevent one branch of government from becoming too powerful is unique, but we have some criticism of it. He recommends that a constitutional convention should be held whenever two branches of government, by a two-thirds vote, desire to change the constitution or correct any violation of it.

Since the people are the source of power in a republican form of government, it would seem logical to consult them whenever one branch becomes too powerful or whenever there is a constitutional crisis. But there are problems in depending upon the people to keep each branch within its constitutional limits.

In the first place, the people cannot prevent the possibility of two branches combining their strength and power against the third branch. The legislative branch, which possesses the most power and influence, could dominate and control the other two branches. Should this happen, the power of the people would be worthless.

In the second place, frequent appeals to the people suggest a serious defect in the government. Such appeals threaten the stability necessary to good government; society is kept in a state of turmoil, and the public peace is destroyed. It is true that this country has been successful in revising its form of government, but we must not become too confident. Too much experimentation can be

82

dangerous. We must remember that the state constitutions were
written at a time when the country was endangered from abroad.
This tended to subdue passions and discord. The citizens felt
united by the Revolution and had confidence in their leaders. But
the Revolution is behind us; divergent views and strong disagree-
ments are coming to the surface.

We know that it is the legislative branch which is most likely
to seize power from the other two branches. The appeals to the
people would, therefore, come from either the executive or judicial
branch. But those branches combined are smaller than the legislative branch, and the people are not as familiar with them. The
judicial branch, in particular, is far removed from the people because justices are appointed, rather than elected, and serve for
life; the people will always view the president with a certain
scepticism; every administration will be subject to a degree of
unpopularity and distortion. By contrast, members of the legislative branch move freely among the people and are connected to them
by ties of blood and friendship. The representatives are elected
by the people and are the most responsive to their wishes. Furthermore, they are regarded as the chief defenders of the peoples'
rights and liberties. For these reasons it is doubtful that the
executive and judicial branches could enlist the sympathies of the
people.

Not only could the legislators plead their cause most successfully, they would dominate the very conventions called to air the
grievances against them.

51

MADISON

To the People of the State of New York:

To what expedient, then, shall we finally resort, for maintaining in practice the necessary partition of power among the several departments, as laid down in the Constitution? The only answer that can be given is, that as all these exterior provisions are found to be inadequate, the defect must be supplied, by so contriving the interior structure of the government as that its several constituent parts may, by their mutual relations, be the means of keeping each other in their proper places. Without presuming to undertake a full development of this important idea, I will hazard a few general observations, which may perhaps place it in a clearer light, and enable us to form a more correct judgment of the principles and structure of the government planned by the convention.

In order to lay a due foundation for that separate and distinct exercise of the different powers of government, which to a certain extent is admitted on all hands to be essential to the preservation of liberty, it is evident that each department should have a will of its own; and consequently should be so constituted that the members of each should have as little agency as possible in the appointment of the members of the others. Were this principle rigorously adhered to, it would require that all the appointments for the supreme executive, legislative, and judiciary magistracies should be drawn from the same fountain of authority, the people, through channels having no communication whatever with one another. Perhaps such a plan of constructing the several departments would be less difficult in practice than it may in contemplation appear. Some difficulties, however, and some additional expense would attend the execution of it. Some deviations, therefore,

84

from the principle must be admitted. In the constitution of the judiciary department in particular, it might be inexpedient to insist rigorously on the principle: first, because peculiar qualifications being essential in the members, the primary consideration ought to be to select that mode of choice which best secures these qualifications; secondly, because the permanent tenure by which the appointments are held in that department, must soon destroy all sense of dependence on the authority conferring them.

It is equally evident, that the members of each department should be as little dependent as possible on those of the others, for the emoluments annexed to their offices. Were the executive magistrate, or the judges, not independent of the legislature in this particular, their independence in every other would be merely nominal.

But the great security against a gradual concentration of the several powers in the same department, consists in giving to those who administer each department the necessary constitutional means and personal motives to resist encroachments of the others. The provision for defence must in this, as in all other cases, be made commensurate to the danger of attack. Ambition must be made to counteract ambition. The interest of the man must be connected with the constitutional rights of the place. It may be a reflection on human nature, that such devices should be necessary to control the abuses of government. But what is government itself, but the greatest of all reflections on human nature? If men were angels, no government would be necessary. If angels were to govern men, neither external nor internal controls on government would be necessary. In framing a government which is to be administered by men over men, the great difficulty lies in this: you must first enable the government to control the governed; and in the next place oblige it to control itself. A dependence on the people is, no doubt, the primary control on the government; but experience has taught mankind the necessity of auxiliary precautions.

This policy of supplying, by opposite and rival interests, the defect of better motives, might be traced through the whole system of human affairs, private as well as public. We see it particularly displayed in all the subordinate distributions of power, where the constant aim is to divide and arrange the several offices in such a manner as that each may be a check on the other--that the private interest of every individual may be a sentinel over the public rights. These inventions of prudence cannot be less requisite in the distribution of the supreme powers of the State.

But it is not possible to give to each department an equal power of self-defence. In republican government, the legislative authority necessarily predominates. The remedy for this inconveniency is to divide the legislature into different branches; and to render them, by different modes of election and different principles of action, as little connected with each other as the nature of their common functions and their common dependence on the society will admit. It may even be necessary to guard against dangerous encroachments by still further precautions. As the weight of the legislative authority requires that it should be thus divided, the weakness of the executive may require, on the other hand, that it should be fortified. An absolute negative on the legislature appears, at first view, to be the natural defence with which the executive magistrate should be armed. But perhaps it would be neither altogether safe nor alone sufficient. On ordinary occasions it might not be exerted with the requisite firmness, and on extraordinary occasions it might be perfidiously abused. May not this defect of an absolute negative be supplied by some qualified connection between this weaker department and the weaker branch of the stronger department, by which the latter may be led to support the constitutional rights of the former, without being too much detached from the rights of its own department?

If the principles on which these observations are founded be just, as I persuade myself they are, and they be applied as a criterion to the several State constitutions, and to the federal

86

Constitution, it will be found that if the latter does not perfectly correspond with them, the former are infinitely less able
to bear such a test.

There are, moreover, two considerations particularly applicable to the federal system of America, which place that system in a
very interesting point of view.

First. In a single republic, all the power surrendered by
the people is submitted to the administration of a single government; and the usurpations are guarded against by a division of the
government into distinct and separate departments. In the compound
republic of America, the power surrendered by the people is first
divided between two distinct governments, and then the portion al-
lotted to each subdivided among distinct and separate departments.
Hence a double security arises to the rights of the people. The
different governments will control each other, at the same time
that each will be controlled by itself.

Second. It is of great importance in a republic not only to
guard the society against the oppression of its rulers, but to
guard one part of the society against the injustice of the other
part. Different interests necessarily exist in different classes
of citizens. If a majority be united by a common interest, the
rights of the minority will be insecure. There are but two methods
of providing against this evil; the one by creating a will in the
community independent of the majority--that is, of the society itself; the other, by comprehending in the society so many separate
descriptions of citizens as will render an unjust combination of a
majority of the whole very improbable, if not impracticable. The
first method prevails in all governments possessing an hereditary
or self-appointed authority. This, at best, is but a precarious
security; because a power independent of the society may as well
espouse the unjust views of the major, as the rightful interests
of the minor party, and may possibly be turned against both parties.
The second method will be exemplified in the federal republic of
the United States. Whilst all authority in it will be derived from

87

and dependent on the society, the society itself will be broken
into so many parts, interests and classes of citizens, that the
rights of individuals, or of the minority, will be in little danger from interested combinations of the majority. In a free government the security for civil rights must be the same as that for
religious rights. It consists in the one case in the multiplicity
of interests, and in the other in the multiplicity of sects. The
degree of security in both cases will depend on the number of interests and sects; and this may be presumed to depend on the extent of country and number of people comprehended under the same
government. This view of the subject must particularly recommend
a proper federal system to all the sincere and considerate friends
of republican government, since it shows that in exact proportion
as the territory of the Union may be formed into more circumscribed
Confederacies, or States, oppressive combinations of a majority
will be facilitated; the best security, under the republican forms,
for the rights of every class of citizens, will be diminished; and
consequently the stability and independence of some member of the
government, the only other security, must be proportionally increased. Justice is the end of government. It is the end of civil
society. It ever has been and ever will be pursued until it be obtained, or until liberty be lost in the pursuit. In a society under the forms of which the stronger faction can readily unite and
oppress the weaker, anarchy may as truly be said to reign as in a
state of nature, where the weaker individual is not secured against
the violence of the stronger; and as, in the latter state, even the
stronger individuals are prompted, by the uncertainty of their condition, to submit to a government which may protect the weak as
well as themselves; so, in the former state, will the more powerful
factions or parties be gradually induced, by a like motive, to wish
for a government which will protect all parties, the weaker as well
as the more powerful. It can be little doubted that if the State
of Rhode Island was separated from the Confederacy and left to itself, the insecurity of rights under the popular form of govern-

88

ment within such narrow limits would be displayed by such reiter-
ated oppressions of factious majorities that some power altogether
independent of the people would soon be called for by the voice of
the very factions whose misrule had proved the necessity of it.
In the extended republic of the United States, and among the great
variety of interests, parties, and sects which it embraces, a coa-
lition of a majority of the whole society could seldom take place
on any other principles than those of justice and the general good;
whilst there being thus less danger to a minor from the will of a
major party, there must be less pretext, also, to provide for the
security of the former, by introducing into the government a will
not dependent on the latter, or, in other words, a will independent
of the society itself. It is no less certain than it is important,
notwithstanding the contrary opinions which have been entertained,
that the larger the society, provided it lie within a practical
sphere, the more duly capable it will be of self-government. And
happily for the *republican cause*, the practicable sphere may be
carried to a very great extent, by a judicious modification and
mixture of the *federal principle*.

PUBLIUS

"IF MEN WERE ANGELS, NO GOVERNMENT WOULD BE NECESSARY."

JAMES MADISON

It is agreed that power ought to be divided among the three branches of government and that each branch should be able to check the power of the other two. The purpose of this Paper is to help you understand how the structure of the proposed government makes this possible.

Each branch should be, in large part, independent. To assure such independence, no one branch should have too much power in selecting members of the other two branches. If this principle were strictly followed, it would mean that the citizens should select the president, the legislators, and the judges. But, though the people are the source of governmental power, the framers recognized certain practical difficulties in making every office elective. In particular, the judicial branch would suffer if its members were selected by the people, because the average person is not aware of the qualifications judges ought to possess. A great deal of thought was given to the method of selecting judges. Not only should judges have great ability, they should also be free of political pressures. Since federal judges are to be appointed for life (subject to good behavior), their thinking will not be influenced by the president who will appoint them, or the senators whose advice and consent the president will seek.

The members of each branch should not be too dependent on the members of the other two branches in the determination of their salaries. If the president, or the judges, had to look to the Congress for salary increases (during their terms of office), or feared that their salaries would be decreased, their independence would be hollow indeed.

The best security against a gradual concentration of power in any one branch is to provide constitutional safeguards which would make such concentration difficult. For instance, the power to provide for adequate defense of the country is an extremely important power, but realizing that some men profit from war, the framers carefully divided the war-making powers. (The power to declare war and to raise money for the military is granted to the Congress; the power to make war and to command the army and navy is granted to the president.) One man's personal interests and ambitions must be checked by the constitutional rights of all. We may not like to admit that men abuse power, but the very need for government itself proves that they do. "If men were angels, no government would be necessary."

All men are imperfect, the rulers and the ruled; consequently, the great problem in framing a government is this: the government must be able to control the people, but equally important, it must be forced to control itself. The dependence of the government on the will of the people is undoubtedly the best control, but experience teaches us that other controls are necessary.

Dividing power helps to check its growth in any one direction, but power cannot be divided absolutely equally. In the republican form of government, the legislative branch tends to be the most powerful. That is why the framers divided the Congress into two branches, the House of Representatives and the Senate, and provided for a different method of election in each branch. Further safeguards against legislative tyranny may be necessary. If the balance of power should shift too markedly to the legislative branch, the executive branch will have to be strengthened. A simple solution might be to provide an absolute presidential veto over legislative acts, but such a solution might not be either altogether safe or sufficient. That is, such a veto might not be exercised when needed or, at the other extreme, it might be used too frequently. The promotion of close ties between the president and the weaker branch of the Congress, the Senate, might prove to be the best solution.

It may be that the proposed Constitution does not perfectly

reflect these principles, but it comes much closer than the state constitutions in setting up safeguards against a monopoly of power.

Certain unique features of the proposed federal system will help to prevent abuse of power. Power, under the Constitution, is first divided between the states and the national government, and again divided by the three branches of the national government. Consequently, the proposed government will provide double security for the rights of the people. In a unitary republic (a country not divided into states), all the power surrendered by the people goes to the national government, and the only protection against abuse of that power is the division of the national government into several branches.

In a representative democracy it is not only important to guard against the oppression of rulers, it is equally important to guard against the injustice which may be inflicted by certain citizens or groups. Majorities often threaten the rights of minorities. There are only two methods of avoiding this evil. One method (we find this in hereditary monarchies) is to construct a powerful government, one that is viewed by the citizens as having a "community will." Such a "will" is larger than, and independent of, the simple majority. This "solution" could be dangerous because such a government might throw its power and weight behind a group in society working against the public good. But in our country, the authority to govern comes from the whole society--the people themselves. In addition, our society is divided into many groups of people who hold different views and have different interests. This makes it very difficult for one group to dominate or threaten the minority groups. Individual rights are safest in societies that contain many classes, just as religious freedom is best protected by the existence of many religious denominations.

Justice is the purpose of government and civil society. If government allows or encourages strong groups to combine together against the weak, liberty will be lost and anarchy will result. And the condition of anarchy tempts even strong individuals and

92

groups to submit to _any_ form of government, no matter how bad, which they hope will protect _them_ as well as the weak.

We can conclude that self-government flourishes best in a large country containing many different groups. _Some_ countries are too large for self-government, but the proposed plan before you modifies the federal principle just enough to make self-government both possible and practical in the United States.

THE HOUSE OF REPRESENTATIVES

52

MADISON

The last four Papers were general in nature. Now I would like to examine more closely the three branches of the proposed new government. I shall begin with the House of Representatives.

After the framers established a House of Representatives, they were faced with two very important questions: who shall decide the qualifications necessary to vote for national representatives and what qualifications should representatives possess. The first question is concerned with the right of suffrage (who shall vote), and the second is concerned with the kind of man best suited to serve in the House. The right of suffrage is one of the most fundamental principles of republican government, so the framers lost no time in defining this right. After considerable deliberation, they decided that the men in each of the thirteen states now qualified to vote for their state representatives will be qualified to vote for national representatives. In most of the states, the qualifications for voting are established in the state constitutions, not the state legislatures, and this seems to me to be quite proper.

The framers could have granted Congress or the state legislatures the power to determine voting qualifications. Or they could have written into the Constitution one uniform rule governing eligibility to vote. Why did they decide the way they did? If Congress had been granted this power it would mean that those elected would have the authority to decide who should elect them! This would be ludicrous. If the framers had allowed the state legislatures to define suffrage rights, the national government would be too dependent upon the states. Also, keep in mind that provisions in the state constitutions are harder to change than acts of the state legislatures. In theory, the state legislatures could change

94

the provision for suffrage set in state constitutions, but state legislators will be reluctant to tamper with rights granted them by the federal Constitution. If the framers had established one uniform set of qualifications, there is no doubt that the states would have objected. Consequently, allowing the states, in their constitutions, to establish the voting qualifications seemed the best compromise.

However, the personal qualifications of the representative are another matter. Congressional representatives will hold a national office, so there should be no objection to uniform qualifications. The Constitution, therefore, requires that a representative of the United States must be at least twenty-five years old; must have been for seven years a citizen of the United States; must, at the time of his election, be an inhabitant of the state he is to represent; and, during the time of his service, must hold no other office in the government. These limitations are reasonable.

Another problem was the length of time the representative should hold office. The framers discussed and debated the two year term. If it is true that the government in general should represent the interests of the people, it is especially true concerning the House of Representatives. Frequent elections are a necessity, but the question faced was, how frequent? Let us, like the framers, consult experience.

Representative government, as opposed to pure or direct democracy, was hardly known in the distant past. We must turn to more modern times to find examples; the House of Commons in Great Britain provides us with the best example. The history of the House of Commons prior to the Magna Charta is obscure; in fact, some historians question whether there even was a House of Commons before 1215, the date of Magna Charta. Records of a later date prove that Parliaments were to be in session every year, not that they were to be elected every year. And even these annual sessions were controlled by the king; under various pretexts, kings contrived

95

long intermissions. The fact that the king could control Parliament in this fashion was a serious threat to the liberties of Englishmen and, to remedy this grievance, a law was passed in the reign of Charles II which provided that parliamentary recesses could not be prolonged beyond three years. During the reign of William III (after a revolution took place) it was declared that holding frequent sessions of Parliament was among the fundamental rights of the people. A few years later Parliament, by statute, tightened the law even more by defining "frequently." This statute provided that a new Parliament must be called no later than three years after the termination of the former. Later on, the law changed once more, from three to seven years. So we can conclude that, in England, a term of three years was considered adequate to keep the representatives accountable to the people. Under our Constitution, which is superior to the English, we can be confident that holding elections every two years is sufficient.

But let us put aside British history for a moment and consider our own country. Before the Revolution, the colonies established the principle of representation in the colonial legislatures. The frequency of elections varied from one to seven years. Virginia, the first state to resist the power of the king and the first to adopt the Declaration of Independence, held elections to the legislature every seven years. I mention this as further proof that elections held every two years can in no way endanger the liberties of the people.

It is important to remember that under the new government legislative power will not be absolute; the Congress will not only be dependent upon the people, it will share its power with the several state legislatures.

And, finally, under the proposed government, neither the president or the judiciary will have sufficient power to influence the House of Representatives in ways that would adversely affect the people.

62

MADISON (?)

This Paper will examine four points concerning the Senate: (1) the qualifications of the senators; (2) the method by which they are selected; (3) equal representation in the Senate; and (4) the number of senators and the six year term.

There are two fundamental differences between the qualifications of senators and representatives: senators must be older (thirty years as opposed to twenty-five for representatives) and must be citizens of the United States longer (nine years as opposed to seven years for representatives). Senators serve longer and need a broader knowledge of government affairs, particularly in the area of foreign relations; consequently, the framers thought they ought to be older. A longer period of citizenship is considered necessary to prevent those senators born outside the United States from being influenced by the politics and habits of their native countries.

Appointment by the state legislatures, rather than election by the people, is desirable for two reasons: (1) appointment best assures that the Senate will consist of a select group of men, and (2) appointment by the states will provide a link between the states and the national government.

The Constitution provides for two senators from each state. This equality of representation is clearly a compromise between the different interests of the large and small states. In a federal system (where power is shared between the states and the national government), it would be unfair not to recognize two opposing principles—proportional versus equal representation. The principle of proportional representation (representation based on population) is recognized in the House; the principle of equal representation is recognized in the Senate. Equal representation in the Senate pro-

97

tects the sovereignty of all the states, whether small or large,
and ought to allay any fear that the new government will abolish
the state governments. Even the large states should not be dis-
tressed by equal representation in the Senate because they, also,
want the states to remain as independent political entities. There
is another advantage in providing for equal representation in the
Senate. In one sense this means that a bill, which must be passed
by both houses before it becomes a law, will reflect the wishes of
the people (who are directly represented in the House) and the
states (directly represented in the Senate).

The method of appointing the senators will tend to solve
another important problem. Frequently, men who hold public office
forget their obligations to the people and betray their public
trust. By dividing the legislative branch into two parts and re-
quiring agreement between them, the liberties of the people will
be more secure, and the passage of bad laws will be more difficult.

The history of governments all over the world demonstrates
that where the legislative body is not divided the legislators
are often swayed by partisan leaders. The Senate, which will consist of fewer men who will hold their office for six years, will
reduce this threat. Representatives, who will be elected by the
people, will serve for only two years; in many cases their private
occupations may be more important to them than their public office,
and they cannot be expected to devote sufficient time to the art
of government or to a study of the laws. Most blunders of our governments to date have been caused by incompetence and a lack of
political wisdom. The Senate ought to go far to correct this situation.

The Senate will not only provide stability in government, it
will reduce the tendency of the House to pass too many laws on too
many subjects. Unnecessary legislation produces chaos and favors
the wealthy. The people cannot be expected to keep up with too
many new laws and regulations; farmers and merchants will be reluctant to start new business ventures if they feel that new laws and

98

regulations will hurt their investments or if they do not understand the laws already on the books.

The object of good government is the happiness of the people,
but good intentions are not enough. Our state and national governments have paid too little attention to statecraft and the art of
government. Fortunately, the structure of the government under
the Constitution will help to correct this defect. A society cannot progress unless the government is both stable and respectable.

To the People of the State of New York:

It is a just and not a new observation, that enemies to particular persons, and opponents to particular measures, seldom confine their censures to such things only in either as are worthy of blame. Unless on this principle, it is difficult to explain the motives of their conduct, who condemn the proposed Constitution in the aggregate, and treat with severity some of the most unexceptionable articles in it.

The second section gives power to the President, *"by and with the advice and consent of the Senate, to make treaties,* PROVIDED TWO THIRDS OF THE SENATORS PRESENT CONCUR."

The power of making treaties is an important one, especially as it relates to war, peace, and commerce; and it should not be delegated but in such a mode, and with such precautions, as will afford the highest security that it will be exercised by men the best qualified for the purpose, and in the manner most conducive to the public good. The convention appears to have been attentive to both these points; they have directed the President to be chosen by select bodies of electors, to be deputed by the people for that express purpose; and they have committed the appointment of senators to the State legislatures. This mode has, in such cases, vastly the advantage of elections by the people in their collective capacity, where the activity of party zeal, taking advantage of the supineness, the ignorance, and the hopes and fears of the unwary and interested, often places men in office by the votes of a small proportion of the electors.

As the select assemblies for choosing the President, as well as the State legislatures who appoint the senators, will in general be composed of the most enlightened and respectable citizens, there is reason to presume that their attention and their votes will be directed to those men only who have become the most distinguished by their abilities and virtue, and in whom the people perceive just grounds for confidence. The Constitution manifests very particular attention to this object. By excluding men under thirty-five from the first office, and those under thirty from the second, it confines the electors to men of whom the people have had time to form a judgment, and with respect to whom they will not be liable to be deceived by those brilliant appearances of genius and patriotism, which, like transient meteors, some times mislead as well as dazzle. If the observation be well founded, that wise kings will always be served by able ministers, it is fair to argue, that as an assembly of select electors possess, in a greater degree than kings, the means of extensive and accurate information relative to men and characters, so will their appointments bear at least equal marks of discretion and discernment. The inference which naturally results from these considerations is this, that the President and senators so chosen will always be of the number of those who best understand our national interests, whether considered in relation to the several States or to foreign nations, who are best able to promote those interests, and whose reputation for integrity inspires and merits confidence. With such men the power of making treaties may be safely lodged.

Although the absolute necessity of system, in the conduct of any business, is universally known and acknowledged, yet the high importance of it in national affairs has not yet become sufficiently impressed on the public mind. They who wish to commit the power under consideration to a popular assembly, composed of members constantly coming and going in quick succession, seem not to recollect that such a body must necessarily be inadequate to the attainment of those great objects, which require to be steadily contemplated in all their relations and circumstances, and which can only be approached and achieved by measures which not only talents, but also exact information, and often much time, are necessary to concert and to execute. It was wise, therefore, in the convention to provide, not only that the power of making treaties should be committed to able and honest men, but also that they should continue in place a sufficient time to become perfectly acquainted with our national concerns, and to form and introduce a system for the management of them. The duration prescribed is such as will give them an opportunity of greatly extending their political information, and of rendering their accumulating experience more and more beneficial to their country. Nor has the convention discovered less prudence in providing for the frequent elections of senators in such a way as to obviate the inconvenience of periodically transferring those great affairs entirely to new men; for by leaving a considerable residue of the old ones in place, uniformity and order, as well as a constant succession of official information, will be preserved.

There are a few who will not admit that the affairs of trade and navigation should be regulated by a system cautiously formed and steadily pursued; and that both our treaties and our laws should correspond with and be made to promote it. It is of much consequence that this correspondence and conformity be carefully maintained; and they who assent to the truth of this position will see and confess that it is well provided for by making concurrence of the Senate necessary both to treaties and to laws.

It seldom happens in the negotiation of treaties, of whatever nature, but that perfect *secrecy* and immediate *despatch* are sometimes requisite. There are cases where the most useful intelligence may be obtained, if the persons possessing it can be relieved from apprehensions of discovery. Those apprehensions will operate on those persons whether they are actuated by mercenary or friendly motives; and there doubtless are many of both descriptions, who would rely on the secrecy of the President, but who would not confide in that of the Senate, and still less in that of a large popular Assembly. The convention have done well, therefore, in so

102

disposing of the power of making treaties, that although the President must, in forming them, act by the advice and consent of the Senate, yet he will be able to manage the business of intelligence in such a manner as prudence may suggest.

They who have turned their attention to the affairs of men, must have perceived that there are tides in them; tides very irregular in their duration, strength, and direction, and seldom found to run twice exactly in the same manner or measure. To discern and to profit by these tides in national affairs is the business of those who preside over them; and they who have had much experience on this head inform us, that there frequently are occasions when days, nay, even when hours, are precious. The loss of a battle, the death of a prince, the removal of a minister, or other circumstances intervening to change the present posture and aspect of affairs, may turn the most favorable tide into a course opposite to our wishes. As in the field, so in the cabinet, there are moments to be seized as they pass, and they who preside in either should be left in capacity to improve them. So often and so essentially have we heretofore suffered from the want of secrecy and despatch, that the Constitution would have been inexcusably defective, if no attention had been paid to those objects. Those matters which in negotiations usually require the most secrecy and the most despatch, are those preparatory and auxiliary measures which are not otherwise important in a national view, than as they tend to facilitate the attainment of the objects of the negotiation. For these, the President will find no difficulty to provide; and should any circumstance occur which requires the advice and consent of the Senate, he may at any time convene them. Thus we see that the Constitution provides that our negotiations for treaties shall have every advantage which can be derived from talents, information, integrity, and deliberate investigations, on the one hand, and from secrecy and despatch on the other.

But to this plan, as to most others that have ever appeared, objections are contrived and urged.

Some are displeased with it, not on account of any errors or defects in it, but because, as the treaties, when made, are to have the force of laws, they should be made only by men invested with legislative authority. These gentlemen seem not to consider that the judgments of our courts, and the commissions constitutionally given by our governor, are as valid and as binding on all persons whom they concern, as the laws passed by our legislature. All constitutional acts of power, whether in the executive or in the judicial department, have as much legal validity and obligation as if they proceeded from the legislature; and therefore, whatever name be given to the power of making treaties, or however obligatory they may be when made, certain it is, that the people may, with much propriety, commit the power to a distinct body from the legislature, the executive, or the judicial. It surely does not follow, that because they have given the power of making laws to the legislature, that therefore they should likewise give them power to do every other act of sovereignty by which the citizens are to be bound and affected.

Others, though content that treaties should be made in the mode proposed, are averse to their being the *supreme* laws of the land. They insist, and profess to believe, that treaties like acts of assembly, should be repealable at pleasure. This idea seems to be new and peculiar to this country, but new errors, as well as new truths, often appear. These gentlemen would do well to reflect that a treaty is only another name for a bargain, and that it would be impossible to find a nation who would make any bargain with us, which should be binding on them *absolutely*, but on us only so long and so far as we may think proper to be bound by it. They who make laws may, without doubt, amend or repeal them; and it will not be disputed that they who make treaties may alter or cancel them; but still let us not forget that treaties are made, not by only one of the contracting parties, but by both; and consequently, that as the consent of both was essential to their formation at first, so must it ever afterwards be to alter

or cancel them. The proposed Constitution, therefore, has not in
the least extended the obligation of treaties. They are just as
binding, and just as far beyond the lawful reach of legislative
acts now, as they will be at any future period, or under any form
of government.

However useful jealousy may be in republics, yet when like
bile in the natural, it abounds too much in the body politic, the
eyes of both become very liable to be deceived by the delusive appearances which that malady casts on surrounding objects. From
this cause, probably, proceed the fears and apprehensions of some,
that the President and Senate may make treaties without an equal
eye to the interests of all the States. Others suspect that two
thirds will oppress the remaining third, and ask whether those
gentlemen are made sufficiently responsible for their conduct;
whether, if they act corruptly, they can be punished; and if they
make disadvantageous treaties, how are we to get rid of those
treaties?

As all the States are equally represented in the Senate, and
by men the most able and the most willing to promote the interests
of their constituents, they will all have an equal degree of influence in that body, especially while they continue to be careful
in appointing proper persons, and to insist on their punctual attendance. In proportion as the United States assume a national
form and a national character, so will the good of the whole be
more and more an object of attention, and the government must be
a weak one indeed, if it should forget that the good of the whole
can only be promoted by advancing the good of each of the parts or
members which compose the whole. It will not be in the power of
the President and Senate to make any treaties by which they and
their families and estates will not be equally bound and affected
with the rest of the community; and, having no private interests
distinct from that of the nation, they will be under no tempta-
tions to neglect the latter.

As to corruption, the case is not supposable. He must either

105

have been very unfortunate in his intercouse with the world, or possess a heart very susceptible of such impressions, who can think it probable that the President and two thirds of the Senate will ever be capable of such unworthy conduct. The idea is too gross and too invidious to be entertained. But in such a case, if it should ever happen, the treaty so obtained from us would, like all other fraudulent contracts, be null and void by the law of nations.

With respect to their responsibility, it is difficult to conceive how it could be increased. Every consideration that can influence the human mind, such as honor, oaths, reputations, conscience, the love of country, and family affections and attachments, afford security for their fidelity. In short, as the Constitution has taken the utmost care that they shall be men of talents, and integrity, we have reason to be persuaded that the treaties they make will be as advantageous as, all circumstances considered, could be made; and so far as the fear of punishment and disgrace can operate, that motive to good behavior is amply afforded by the article on the subject of impeachments.

PUBLIUS

JAY

The treaty-making power is an important power especially when the subject of treaties has to do with war and peace or trade relations among nations. Such a power should not be delegated lightly --and it has not been. The Constitution provides that the president may enter into treaties with foreign nations, but he must not only seek "the advice and consent of the Senate," two-thirds of the senators present must concur. (Article II, section 2)

Both the president and the senators will be indirectly selected by the people; this screening process will assure us that the men to whom such an important power is delegated will be qualified to exercise it on behalf of the public good. There is every reason to assume that the senators and the president will be in the best position to define our national interests, will be able to promote those interests most effectively, and will inspire confidence in the people.

Some people think the treaty-making power should be lodged in the House of Representatives. We do not agree. Representatives will be elected every two years; they will be continually coming and going and will not have the time to study the terms of the treaties before them or have the experience to master the complexities of our foreign policy. Senators, on the other hand, will hold their office for six years and their terms are staggered. There will always be men of considerable experience in the Senate, men who on a day-to-day basis are actively involved in the making of foreign policy.

Both secrecy and speed are often necessary in the negotiation of treaties. There will be times when it will be vital to obtain information from people, matters pertaining to foreign intelligence, and people who possess this important information may be

unwilling to confide in the Senate. They will be less reluctant
to trust one man, the president. At the same time you need not
fear that the management of foreign affairs or the negotiation of
treaties will be the monopoly of the president since the final
form of the treaty will have to be approved by two-thirds of the
Senate.

There are "tides" in the affairs of men. These tides, like
the ocean's tides, vary in their duration, strength, and direction.
Just as the fisherman must know the tides of the sea, so also must
men in public life be able to discern and profit from the changing
tides of political life. How quickly the tides, both of the sea
and of human events, change! A man is removed from public office,
a prince dies, a battle is lost--the tide has changed and the moment must be seized. The framers of our Constitution understood
this phenomenon in nature and in man. In order to act upon these
changing tides of human affairs, these accidents of history, the
framers granted the president sufficient power to take the initiative in the treaty-making process. The treaty-making power is a
beautifully balanced one; secrecy and quick execution on the part
of the president will be balanced by the careful deliberations of
the Senate. The president will be able to act decisively, but he
will be prevented from acting irresponsibly.

Still, there are the inevitable objections. Treaties, it is
argued, will have the force of laws and should, therefore, be made
by the legislative branch only. Those who argue this way forget
that decisions of the courts and rulings by executive commissions
and bureaus are as binding as legislative acts. It is true that
the law-making functions are granted to the legislature, but citizens are (and will be) as bound by executive and judicial acts as
laws passed by the Congress. We also hear that treaties should
not be part of the supreme law of the land. These people think
that treaties, like laws passed by Congress, should be repealable
at any time. But remember that treaties are simply bargains between nations; what nation would make a bargain with us knowing

that they are bound absolutely to the terms of that bargain but that we could violate that bargain at our whim? Both parties to a treaty should agree to any change or cancellation.

Too much jealousy and cynicism at large in the body politic, like too much bile in the physical body, results in distorted vision. This condition best explains the fear of some people that the president and Senate will make treaties which may hurt the interests of specific states. These people should keep in mind that the states are equally represented in the Senate and that the senators themselves will be as bound by the terms of treaties as other citizens. We must all realize that the best interests of the nation are greater than the interests of the individual states. We are, after all, establishing a national government.

Another objection frequently voiced is that two-thirds of the senators will oppress the remaining third or that they may act irresponsibly and enter into treaties disadvantageous to our interests. We hear also that the senators may act corruptly and if they do, the question is asked, can they be punished? I think these objections have been answered--with the exception of corruption. How can anyone think that the president and two-thirds of the Senate would ever deliberately conspire against the nation's interests? Such an idea is too gross to be entertained! But should it ever happen, this corruption and conspiracy, the treaty obtained in this manner would be considered a fraudulent contract and would never stand up under the law of nations. If any other doubts remain or if further proof is needed that the welfare of the country will not be betrayed by those entrusted with the treaty-making power, we refer you to the power of impeachment.

65

HAMILTON

The Constitution grants two other important powers to the Senate. The first of these powers, the power to appoint men to public office, is shared with the president and has already been discussed. This Paper is concerned with the Senate's power to act as the trial court in impeachment cases.

The entire impeachment process involves a <u>national inquest</u> into the conduct of public men. An impeachable offense involves official misconduct, not in the usual sense of that word, but in the sense of an abuse of power or violation of public trust. Such offenses are uniquely <u>political</u> in nature because the entire society suffers the consequences. For this reason, impeachment trials will excite and agitate many citizens; people will take sides and public discussion will be charged with emotion. Fair and objective evaluation will be very difficult.

The framers felt that the inquisitors for the nation should be the representatives of the people. For that reason both houses of Congress are involved in the impeachment process. The House of Representatives determines whether or not sufficient evidence exists to indict (charge with an impeachable offense). If the House votes impeachment, its role in the impeachment process ends. The Senate tries the case and will either vote to acquit or convict the person impeached.

The impeachment court should be qualified for its special function. The framers, after considerable deliberation, concluded that the Senate will have the necessary dignity, independence, and confidence to act as the impeachment court. Because senators will be indirectly elected they will be able to remain objective and impartial; they will stand between the person impeached and his accusers, the representatives.

Some people have suggested that the Supreme Court should try impeachment cases. Why, they ask, did the framers turn instead to the legislative branch to form a court? One reason is that the framers felt that the Supreme Court justices might be reluctant to disagree with the findings of the House; such reluctance, quite obviously, would be unfair to the person impeached. Also, the citizens will have strong opinions concerning the impeachment of a particular person; the Senate will have greater authority and popularity than the Supreme Court and will, therefore, be better able to convince the people that its verdict is the proper one. To enlarge the court (add more judges for impeachment cases) might help to qualify the Supreme Court as the proper impeachment court, but this would be impractical. These reasons are sufficient to eliminate the Supreme Court as the appropriate tribunal for impeachment trials, but there is another important reason: a person impeached and convicted "can no longer hold any office of honor, trust, or profit under the United States;" he loses the esteem he once enjoyed and, in addition, is still liable to prosecution, conviction, and punishment for any criminal (as opposed to political) acts he may have committed while in office. This means that those convicted of impeachment by the Supreme Court might find themselves back on trial on criminal charges in the same court! The very men who took away honor and respect in the impeachment trial could, in a second trial, take away life!

The framers decided it was inadvisable to combine the Supreme Court and the Senate to form an impeachment court; they found it equally inadvisable to establish a court of impeachment composed of men unconnected with any branch of the national government. A court consisting of men drawn from state governments might be influenced by factious or political interests or by a powerful majority in the House of Representatives. And, finally, it would be impractical to maintain a special and permanent court whose sole purpose is to try impeachment cases.

But even if you think some other plan is better, it does not

111

follow that the <u>entire</u> Constitution should be rejected. We risk
the possibility of anarchy if perfection is demanded in every specific area of government. Opponents of the Constitution have the
responsibility of proving that the entire plan of government will
be injurious to the public good.

67

HAMILTON

This Paper will comment on certain arguments raised against the proposed Executive branch.

The Executive is the most criticized branch of the proposed government, but the arguments of the anti-Federalists are weak and lack sound judgment. It seems as though they deliberately misrepresent what the Constitution actually says. They play heavily on the fear of monarchy and hint that the president will develop into a despot equal to any king. They stop at nothing in an attempt to develop their arguments; some even turn to fiction to try to illustrate their points. From some of their writing we conjure up scenes of murderous and terrifying Turkish troops surrounding the president; he is described wearing a crown and seated on a throne in a place resembling a sultan's palace!

These fantastic and irresponsible exaggerations must be countered by a sober and rational discussion of the president's powers. Otherwise, these distortions and dramatics will frighten the people and make it impossible for them to judge the true nature of the Executive branch of government. A certain amount of partisanship concerning the Constitution is to be expected, but the kind of opposition described exceeds partisan politics. For example, one anti-Federalist tells us that the president will have the power to fill vacancies in the Senate. This is an outrageous claim. Article 1, section 3, of the Constitution states:

> The Senate of the United States shall be composed of two Senators from each State, chosen by the Legislature thereof, for six years; and each Senator shall have one vote.

If a senator dies or resigns while the state legislature is in recess, the governor of the state may make a temporary appointment "until the next meeting of the legislature, which shall then fill such vacancies." (Article 1, section 3) The language of the Constitution is clear.

It is difficult not to conclude that the author of such nonsense set out consciously to distort the Constitution and mislead the people.

THE METHOD OF ELECTING THE PRESIDENT

68

HAMILTON

The method of selecting the president is the only significant provision in the Constitution that has not been severely criticized.
In fact, one of the anti-Federalists has admitted that the method
of selecting the president will make it difficult for the president
to abuse the power of his office. I go even further; if the method
of selection is not perfect, it is at least excellent.

A few men, carefully selected by their fellow-citizens, will
be the most likely to understand the qualities needed in a Chief
Executive. They will deliberate under conditions favorable to a
good choice because the electors will be selected in each state
and will assemble and vote in their respective states (not in one
collective body). Therefore, they will be able to exercise independent judgment. If they were allowed to meet at one time and in
one place partisan politics would be difficult to control. Consequently, the possibility of civic disorder is reduced by the
method of indirect election.

There are other reasons to prefer indirect election; foreign
governments, trying to gain power or influence in America, will
find it difficult to corrupt a few highly qualified electors. Such
influence and corruption would be harder to control if the citizens
voted directly, or if the selection of the president were made by
a permanent group of men or by one branch of the government. A
further safeguard is that no man holding a government position can
be chosen as an elector. To assure that qualified men will be selected as president and to prevent foreign corruption and intrigue,
the framers rely upon the following four Constitutional provisions:

      1.   The electors change with every presidential "election."
      2.   The electors have nothing to gain personally by the
           selection they make.

3. The president must be a native born citizen.

4. The Executive branch is separate and independent.

It is possible that a clever and dishonest politician may be elected governor of a state, but such a man will be unable to deceive the presidential electors. The Constitution establishes such an excellent Executive branch and method of presidential selection that we recommend its adoption on this basis alone.

The same method will be used to select the vice-president, except that in case of a tie in the votes cast by the electors, the Senate (instead of the House) will "elect" him. Many people contend that the Senate should select the vice-president from among its own members. It would, however, be awkward if he were selected from that body because one of the duties of the vice-president is to preside over the Senate (Article I, section 3). This duty and power is an example of one of the checks and balances so carefully written into the Constitution. Another objection to selecting one of the senators to serve as vice-president is that since the latter may become the president the same method of selection should be used.

HAMILTON

This Paper will examine the nature of the Presidency. The opposition to the Executive branch is particularly severe and unfair.

The most striking feature to be noted is that the power of the Executive, with few exceptions, is vested in one man. But this fact should not frighten people into thinking that the framers have established a monarchy. There is no resemblance between the proposed president and the king of England.

The president is to be elected for a term of four years, but there is no limit on the number of times he may be reelected. This is in direct opposition to the practice in hereditary monarchies; in England, for example, the king inherits his power and passes it on to his heirs. The American Presidency can, however, be compared to the governorship of New York; the governor of this state is elected for three years and can be reelected without limitation. Actually, it is much easier to establish dangerous influence in a single state than throughout the entire country; therefore, the three year term for governor should cause more apprehension than a four year term for the president.

The Constitution provides for impeachment of the president. If the president is impeached and convicted, he is to be removed from office and can be tried for any crimes he may have committed while in office. The king of England is immune from any such law; there is no branch of government or court to which he is answerable. In fact, any punishment to which the king might be subjected would undoubtedly result in civil unrest or revolution. The president, in contrast, will be held accountable for his actions; he will have no more power than the governor of New York and considerably less power than the governors of Maryland and Delaware.

The Constitution grants the president a <u>limited</u> veto power.

He can return a bill for reconsideration, but if his veto is over-
ridden by a two-thirds vote of both houses of Congress it becomes
law. The king of England has an absolute veto. Just because the
king does not often exercise his veto power simply means that he
has managed to replace his authority with influence. The king is
intelligent enough to know that to exercise the veto too often
might result in a certain degree of political instability.

The president is to be the commander-in-chief of the army and
navy, but he cannot declare war or raise and regulate fleets and
armies as the English king may do; these powers, under the American
Constitution, belong to the legislative branch. It is true that
the governor of New York has power under the state constitution to
take command of the state militia only, but several state constitutions vest their governors with the power of commander-in-chief of
the army and navy as well. It could be argued that the governors
of New Hampshire and Massachusetts, for instance, have greater
power in this respect than the proposed Constitution confers upon
the president of the United States! The president is granted extensive pardoning power, but that power does not extend in cases
of impeachment. Since the president cannot pardon those who have
been impeached, he cannot protect those who plot or conspire
against the government. The president can adjourn Congress only
in cases of disagreement over the time of adjournment, while the
English king may postpone or even dissolve the Parliament; the
governor of New York also has the power to discontinue or postpone
sessions of the state legislature.

The president shares the treaty-making power with the Senate,
while the king of England has sole power in the area of foreign
affairs. It has recently been hinted that the king's authority in
foreign affairs is shared with Parliament, but there is no evidence
to support this contention. The great jurist, Blackstone, and
other experts on the British constitution know that the king's authority in negotiating treaties, forming alliances, etc., is absolute. Sometimes Parliament changes existing laws to conform to

118

the provisions in a new treaty, but that does not justify the conclusion that the king and Parliament share power in the area of
foreign affairs.

The president is to have the power "to receive ambassadors
and other public ministers," but this is not a matter of power and
authority; rather, it is a matter of dignity and symbol. It would
be inconvenient (and a little foolish) to have to convene Congress
every time a foreign minister arrived!

The president is to have the power, with the advice and consent of the Senate, to appoint ambassadors and other public ministers, Supreme Court justices, and other officers of the United
States whose appointments are not otherwise provided for by the
Constitution. Contrast the president's power of appointment with
that of the English king; the king not only has the sole power to
appoint all officers, he can create offices, confer titles of nobility at his pleasure, and promote members of the clergy.

Except for the president's treaty-making power (and that is a
shared power), it would be difficult to establish that the president will have greater power than the governor of New York has at
present. Even more significant, we have seen that no parallel exists between the power of the American president and that of the
English king. To firmly establish this point, let us take one last
look at the striking differences between the powers of the president and those of the king.

1. The president will be elected by the people for a four
    year term.

        The king of Great Britain is a perpetual and hered-
        itary prince.

2. The president is subject to personal punishment, impeach-
    ment and disgrace.

        The king is sacred and inviolable.

3. The president will have a qualified (or limited) veto.
    A two-thirds vote of the legislature will override his
    veto.

        The king enjoys an absolute veto.

119

4. The president will become commander-in-chief of the armed forces, but unlike the king, cannot declare war or raise armies or navies.

5. The president will share the treaty-making power with the Senate.

    The king has the sole power of making treaties.

6. The president will share the appointment power with the legislative branch.

    The king possesses sole power in the making of appointment.

7. The president cannot grant privileges.

    The king can confer citizenship and titles of nobility.

8. The president has no power to make laws concerning commerce or currency.

    The king has the final say in all commercial matters.

9. The president will have no religious or spiritual authority.

    The king is the symbolic head of the national church.

HAMILTON

Many people think that a vigorous and strong president is incompatible with a republican form of government. We do not agree. An energetic and forceful president is essential to good government.

National defense, sound administration of the law, and the protection of property rights all depend upon the vitality of the Presidency. In addition, an energetic president best protects liberty when it is threatened by faction, anarchy, and the excessive ambitions of others. Anyone familiar with Roman history knows that it was often the Roman dictator who prevented the fall of the country to foreign enemies or domestic citizens. We must assume that sensible men agree that the president should be strong. What, then, constitutes strength and energy? What characteristics do we look for? Can sufficient strength in the Presidency be combined with the principles of republican government?

An energetic Executive branch must be characterized by unity, sufficient powers, and a certain degree of secrecy. For these reasons, one Chief Executive is better than two or more. Two people, granted equal power and authority, are bound to differ. Personal ambition can never be totally subdued, and a dual Presidency would be marked by dissension, weakened authority, and the growth of conflicting factions. It is unnecessary and unwise to establish an Executive branch which would make this form of divisiveness possible. Conflict and argument are dangerous in the Executive branch where decisions must be prompt; in the Congress, on the other hand, differences of opinion force discussion and deliberation. This is quite proper in the legislative branch and helps to prevent coercion by a majority. The function of the legislature is to pass laws; once a law is passed, effective opposition comes to an end. But the Executive branch is charged with the execution of the laws;

121

a law once passed should be executed promptly. Furthermore, in case of war, when so much depends upon a strong Presidency, divisiveness could destroy the national security.

The same arguments against having two presidents can be made in opposition to an Executive council. In either a plural or council form of Executive faults and defects are more easily concealed, and no one person can be held responsible. The American president, unlike the English king, must not be immune from censure, accountability, or punishment. The English king is not held responsible for his administration, and his person is sacred. Sometimes a king forms a council to act as a buffer between him and his subjects. But such a council in no way diminishes the king's power; he is not even bound by the resolutions the council passes. The council functions as a public relations body while, at the same time, it protects the king in his absolute power.

In a republican form of government every public official is responsible for his behavior in office; the British council, therefore, violates one of the most important principles of republicanism. Many of our state constitutions provide for an Executive council; this obviously reflects the fear many people have of power in the hands of one man. I do not agree that power is less dangerous if it is shared by many. It is much easier to keep an eye on one man than on two or more.

Two last points--but I will not dwell on them. First, there is the matter of expense. Those who recommend a council form of Executive admit that the council should be large. That being so, the salaries of the council members would constitute too great an expense for the nation to tolerate. Second, before the Constitution was written, intelligent men agreed that New York's single Executive (one governor) was one of the most admirable features of the state government.

HAMILTON

To the People of the State of New York:

We proceed now to an examination of the judiciary department of the proposed government.

In unfolding the defects of the existing Confederation, the utility and necessity of a federal judicature have been clearly pointed out. It is the less necessary to recapitulate the considerations there urged, as the propriety of the institution in the abstract is not disputed; the only questions which have been raised being relative to the manner of constituting it, and to its extent. To these points, therefore, our observations shall be confined.

The manner of constituting it seems to embrace these several objects: 1st. The mode of appointing the judges. 2d. The tenure by which they are to hold their places. 3d. The partition of the judiciary authority between different courts, and their relations to each other.

First. As to the mode of appointing the judges; this is the same with that of appointing the officers of the Union in general, and has been so fully discussed in the two last numbers, that nothing can be said here which would not be useless repetition.

Second. As to the tenure by which the judges are to hold their places; this chiefly concerns their duration in office; the provisions for their support; the precautions for their responsibility.

According to the plan of the convention, all judges who may be appointed by the United States are to hold their office *during good behavior*; which is conformable to the most approved of the State constitutions, and among the rest, to that of this State. Its propriety having been drawn into question by the adversaries of that plan, is no light symptom of the rage for objection, which disorders their imaginations and judgments. The standard of good behavior for the continuance in office of the judicial magistracy, is certainly one of the most valuable of the modern improvements in the practice of government. In a monarchy it is an excellent barrier to the despotism of the prince; in a republic it is a no less excellent barrier to the encroachments and oppressions of the representative body. And it is the best expedient which can be devised in any government, to secure a steady, upright, and impartial administration of the laws.

Whoever attentively considers the different departments of power must perceive, that, in a government in which they are separated from each other, the judiciary, from the nature of its functions, will always be the least dangerous to the political rights of the Constitution; because it will be least in a capacity to annoy or injure them. The Executive not only dispenses the honors, but holds the sword of the community. The legislature not only commands the purse, but prescribes the rules by which the duties and rights of every citizen are to be regulated. The judiciary, on the contrary, has no influence over either the sword or the purse; no direction either of the strength or of the wealth of the society; and can take no active resolution whatever. It may truly be said to have neither FORCE nor WILL, but merely judgment; and must ultimately depend upon the aid of the executive arm even for the efficacy of its judgments.

This simple view of the matter suggests several important consequences. It proves incontestably, that the judiciary is beyond comparison the weakest of the three departments of power[*]; that it can never attack with success either of the other two; and that all possible care is requisite to enable it to defend itself against their attacks. It equally proves, that though individual

_____

[*] The celebrated Montesquieu, speaking of them, says: "Of the three powers above mentioned, the judiciary is next to nothing." -- "Spirit of Laws," vol. i., page 186. --PUBLIUS

oppression may now and then proceed from the courts of justice, the general liberty of the people can never be endangered from that quarter; I mean so long as the judiciary remains truly distinct from both the legislature and the Executive. For I agree, that "there is no liberty, if the power of judging be not separated from the legislative and executive powers."* And it proves, in the last place, that as liberty can have nothing to fear from the judiciary alone, but would have everything to fear from its union with either of the other departments; that as all the effects of such a union must ensue from a dependence of the former on the latter, notwithstanding a nominal and apparent separation; that as, from the natural feebleness of the judiciary, it is in continual jeopardy of being overpowered, awed, or influenced by its coordinate branches; and that as nothing can contribute so much to its firmness and independence as permanency in office, this quality may therefore be justly regarded as an indispensable ingredient in its constitution, and, in a great measure, as the citadel of the public justice and the public security.

The complete independence of the courts of justice is peculiarly essential in a limited Constitution. By a limited Constitution, I understand one which contains certain specified exceptions to the legislative authority; such, for instance, as that it shall pass no bills of attainder, no *ex-post-facto* laws, and the like. Limitations of this kind can be preserved in practice no other way than through the medium of courts of justice, whose duty it must be to declare all acts contrary to the manifest tenor of the Constitution void. Without this, all the reservations of particular rights or privileges would amount to nothing.

Some perplexity respecting the rights of the courts to pronounce legislative acts void, because contrary to the constitution, has arisen from an imagination that the doctrine would imply a superiority of the judiciary to the legislative power. It is

---

* "Spirit of Laws," vol. i., page 181. --PUBLIUS

urged that the authority which can declare the acts of another
void, must necessarily be superior to the one whose acts may be
declared void. As this doctrine is of great importance in all the
American constitutions, a brief discussion of the ground on which
it rests cannot be unacceptable.

There is no position which depends on clearer principles,
than that every act of a delegated authority, contrary to the ten-
or of the commission under which it is exercised, is void. No
legislative act, therefore, contrary to the Constitution, can be
valid. To deny this, would be to affirm, that the deputy is
greater than his principal; that the servant is above his master;
that the representatives of the people are superior to the people
themselves; that men acting by virtue of powers, may do not only
what their powers do not authorize, but what they forbid.

If it be said that the legislative body are themselves the
constitutional judges of their own powers, and that the construction they put upon them is conclusive upon the other departments,
it may be answered, that this cannot be the natural presumption,
where it is not to be collected from any particular provisions in
the Constitution. It is not otherwise to be supposed, that the
Constitution could intend to enable the representatives of the
people to substitute their *will* to that of their constituents. It
is far more rational to suppose, that the courts were designed to
be an intermediate body between the people and the legislature, in
order, among other things, to keep the latter within the limits
assigned to their authority. The interpretation of the laws is
the proper and peculiar province of the courts. A constitution
is, in fact, and must be regarded by the judges, as a fundamental
law. It therefore belongs to them to ascertain its meaning, as
well as the meaning of any particular act proceeding from the
legislative body. If there should happen to be an irreconcilable
variance between the two, that which has the superior obligation
and validity ought, of course, to be preferred; or, in other words,
the Constitution ought to be preferred to the statute, the inten-

tion of the people to the intention of their agents.

Nor does this conclusion by any means suppose a superiority of the judicial to the legislative power. It only supposes that the power of the people is superior to both; and that where the will of the legislature, declared in its statutes, stands in opposition to that of the people, declared in the Constitution, the judges ought to be governed by the latter rather than the former. They ought to regulate their decisions by the fundamental laws, rather than by those which are not fundamental.

This exercise of judicial discretion, in determining between two contradictory laws, is exemplified in a familiar instance. It not uncommonly happens, that there are two statutes existing at one time, clashing in whole or in part with each other, and neither of them containing any repealing clause or expression. In such a case, it is the province of the courts to liquidate and fix their meaning and operation. So far as they can, by any fair construction, be reconciled to each other, reason and law conspire to dictate that this should be done; where this is impracticable, it becomes a matter of necessity to give effect to one, in exclusion of the other. The rule which has obtained in the courts for determining their relative validity is, that the last in order of time shall be preferred to the first. But this is a mere rule of construction, not derived from any positive law, but from the nature and reason of the thing. It is a rule not enjoined upon the courts by legislative provision, but adopted by themselves, as consonant to truth and propriety, for the direction of their conduct as interpreters of the law. They thought it reasonable, that between the interfering acts of an *equal* authority, that which was the last indication of its will should have the preference.

But in regard to the interfering acts of a superior and subordinate authority, of an original and derivative power, the nature and reason of the thing indicate the converse of that rule as proper to be followed. They teach us that the prior act of a superior ought to be preferred to the subsequent act of an inferior and subordinate authority; and that accordingly, whenever a particular statute contravenes the Constitution, it will be the duty of the judicial tribunals to adhere to the latter and disregard the former.

It can be of no weight to say that the courts, on the pretence of a repugnancy, may substitute their own pleasure to the constitutional intentions of the legislature. This might as well happen in the case of two contradictory statues; or it might as well happen in every adjudication upon any single statute. The courts must declare the sense of the law; and if they should be disposed to exercise WILL instead of JUDGMENT, the consequence would equally be the substitution of their pleasure to that of the legislative body. The observations, if it prove any thing, would prove that there ought to be no judges distinct from that body.

If, then, the courts of justice are to be considered as the bulwarks of a limited Constitution against legislative encroachments, this consideration will afford a strong argument for the permanent tenure of judicial offices, since nothing will contribute so much as this to that independent spirit in the judges which must be essential to the faithful performance of so arduous a duty.

This independence of the judges is equally requisite to guard the Constitution and the rights of individuals from the effects of those ill humors, which the arts of designing men, or the influence of particular conjunctures, sometimes disseminate among the people themselves, and which, though they speedily give place to better information, and more deliberate reflection, have a tendency, in the meantime, to occasion dangerous innovations in the government, and serious oppressions of the minor party in the community. Though I trust the friends of the proposed Constitution will never concur with its enemies,* in questioning that fundamental principle of republican government, which admits the right of the people to alter or abolish the established Constitution, whenever they find

* *Vide* "Protest of the Minority of the Convention of Pennsylvania," Martin's Speech, etc.   --PUBLIUS

it inconsistent with their happiness, yet it is not to be inferred from this principle, that the representatives of the people, whenever a momentary inclination happens to lay hold of a majority of their constituents, incompatible with the provisions in the existing Constitution, would, on that account, be justifiable in a violation of those provisions; or that the courts would be under a greater obligation to connive at infractions in this shape, than when they had proceeded wholly from the cabals of the representative body. Until the people have by some solemn and authoritative act, annulled or changed the established form, it is binding upon themselves collectively, as well as individually; and no presumption, or even knowledge, of their sentiments, can warrant their representatives in a departure from it, prior to such an act. But it is easy to see, that it would require an uncommon portion of fortitude in the judges to do their duty as faithful guardians of the Constitution, where legislative invasions of it had been instigated by the major voice of the community.

But it is not with a view to infractions of the Constitution only, that the independence of the judges may be an essential safeguard against the effects of occasional ill humors in the society. These sometimes extend no farther than to the injury of the private rights of particular classes of citizens, by unjust and partial laws. Here also the firmness of the judicial magistracy is of vast importance in mitigating the severity and confining the operation of such laws. It not only serves to moderate the immediate mischiefs of those which may have been passed but it operates as a check upon the legislative body in passing them; who, perceiving that obstacles to the success of iniquitous intention are to be expected from the scruples of the courts, are in a manner compelled, by the very motives of the injustice they meditate, to qualify their attempts. This is a circumstance calculated to have more influence upon the character of our governments, than but few may be aware of. The benefits of the integrity and moderation of the judiciary have already been felt in more States than one; and

129

though they may have displeased those whose sinister expectations they may have disappointed, they must have commanded the esteem and applause of all the virtuous and disinterested. Considerate men, of every description, ought to prize whatever will tend to beget or fortify that temper in the courts; as no man can be sure that he may not be to-morrow the victim of a spirit of injustice, by which he many be a gainer to-day. And every man must now feel, that the inevitable tendency of such a spirit is to sap the foundations of public and private confidence, and to introduce in its stead universal distrust and distress.

That inflexible and uniform adherence to the rights of the Constitution, and of individuals, which we perceive to be indispensable in the courts of justice, can certainly not be expected from judges who hold their offices by a temporary commission. Periodical appointments, however regulated, or by whomsoever made, would, in some way or other, be fatal to their necessary independence. If the power of making them was committed either to the Executive or legislature, there would be danger of an improper complaisance to the branch which possessed it; if to both, there would be an unwillingness to hazard the displeasure of either; if to the people, or to persons chosen by them for the special purpose, there would be too great a disposition to consult popularity, to justify a reliance that nothing would be consulted but the Constitution and the laws.

There is yet a further and a weightier reason for the permanency of the judicial offices, which is deducible from the nature of the qualifications they require. It has been frequently remarked, with great propriety, that a voluminous code of laws is one of the inconveniences necessarily connected with the advantages of a free government. To avoid an arbitrary discretion in the courts, it is indispensable that they should be bound down by strict rules and precedents, which serve to define and point out their duty in every particular case that comes before them; and it will readily be conceived from the variety of controversies which grow out of the folly and wickedness of mankind, that the records of those precedents must unavoidably swell to a very considerable bulk, and must demand long and laborious study to acquire a competent knowledge of them. Hence it is, that there can be but few men in the society who will have sufficient skill in the laws to qualify them for the stations of judges. And making the proper deductions for the ordinary depravity of human nature, the number must be still smaller of those who unite the requisite integrity with the requisite knowledge. These considerations apprise us, that the government can have no great option between fit character; and that a temporary duration in office, which would naturally discourage such characters from quitting a lucrative line of practice to accept a seat on the bench, would have a tendency to throw the administration of justice into hands less able, and less well qualified, to conduct it with utility and dignity. In the present circumstances of this country, and in those in which it is likely to be for a long time to come, the disadvantages on this score would be greater than they may at first sight appear; but it must be confessed, that they are far inferior to those which present themselves under the other aspects of the subject.

Upon the whole, there can be no room to doubt that the convention acted wisely in copying from the models of those constitutions which have established *good behavior* as the tenure of their judicial offices, in point of duration; and that so far from being blamable on this account, their plan would have been inexcusably defective, if it had wanted this important feature of good government. The experience of Great Britain affords an illustrious comment on the excellence of the institution.

PUBLIUS

131

THE IMPORTANCE OF AN INDEPENDENT JUDICIARY AND
THE MEANING OF JUDICIAL REVIEW

78

HAMILTON

We have already discussed the necessity of establishing a judicial branch of government and the best method of appointing the judges. This Paper will discuss the importance of an independent judicial branch and the meaning of judicial review.

The Constitution proposes that federal judges hold their office for life, subject to good behavior. The fact that there are opponents of this provision proves how irrational some opposition to the Constitution is. There is no question that life tenure for United States judges is one of the most valuable advances in the theory of representative government. Permanency in office frees judges from political pressures and prevents invasions on judicial power by the president and Congress.

The judicial branch of government is the weakest branch. The president, for example, has the power of appointment and is granted extensive war-making power; the legislative branch controls the money and has the greatest influence over the rights and duties of all citizens. The judicial branch, on the other hand, possesses only the power to judge, not to act, and even its judgments or decisions depend upon the executive branch to carry them out. In addition, our political rights are least threatened by the judicial branch. Occasionally, an individual may be unfairly treated by the courts, but liberty, in general, can never be threatened by them.

The Constitution imposes certain restrictions on the Congress designed to protect individual liberties, but unless the courts are independent and have the power to declare laws in violation of the Constitution null and void these protections amount to nothing. The power of the Supreme Court to declare laws unconstitutional leads some people to assume that the judicial branch will be superior to the legislative branch. Let us look at this argument.

Only the Constitution is <u>fundamental</u> law; the Constitution establishes both the principles and structure of the government. To argue that the Constitution is not superior to the laws suggests that the <u>representatives of the people</u> are superior <u>to the people</u> and that the Constitution is inferior to the government it gave birth to. The courts are the arbiters between the legislative branch and the people; the courts are to interpret the laws and prevent the legislative branch from exceeding the powers granted to it. The courts must not only place the Constitution higher than the laws passed by Congress, they must also place the intentions of the people ahead of the intentions of their representatives. This is not a matter of which branch is superior: it is simply to acknowledge that the people are superior to both. It is futile to argue that the court's decisions, in some instances, might interfere with the will of the legislature. People argue that it is the function of Congress, not the courts, to pass laws and formulate policy. This is true, but to interpret the laws and judge their constitutionality are the two special functions of the court. The fact that the courts are charged with determining what the law means does not suggest that they will be justified in substituting <u>their will</u> for that of the Congress.

The independence of the courts is also necessary to protect the rights of individuals against the destructive actions of factions. Certain designing men may influence the legislature to formulate policies and pass laws that violate the Constitution or individual rights. The fact that the people have the right to change or abolish their government if it becomes inconsistent with their happiness is not sufficient protection; in the first place, stability requires that such changes should be orderly and constitutional. A government at the mercy of groups continually plotting its downfall would be a deplorable situation. The only way citizens can feel their rights are secure is to know that the judicial branch protects them against people, both in and outside government, who work against their interests.

There is another important reason judges ought to hold their office for life. In a free government there are bound to be many laws, some of them complex and contradictory. It takes many years to fully understand the meaning of these laws. A short term of office would discourage able and honest men from seeking an appointment to the courts; they would be reluctant to give up lucrative law practices to accept a temporary judicial appointment. Life tenure, modified by good behavior, is a superb device for assuring judicial independence and protection of individual rights.

84

HAMILTON

The previous Papers tried to answer most of the objections to the Constitution, but some objections have not yet been discussed. This Paper will examine them.

The most important of the remaining objections is that the Constitution does not contain a bill of rights. It has already been pointed out that several state constitutions do not contain bills of rights, including New York state. Oddly enough, New York citizens who oppose the federal Constitution on the ground that it does not contain a bill of rights have tremendous admiration for the state constitution. These citizens claim that the state constitution does not need a separate bill of rights because the guarantee of individual rights is written into the constitution itself. The same is true of the federal Constitution.

As we have seen, many safeguards against the abuse of power are built into the structure of the national government, such as the separation of powers and checks and balances. In this Paper we will list and examine certain other provisions designed to protect individual liberties. Six provisions are particularly significant:

1.   To protect the people against executive and judicial abuse of power, the Constitution provides the power to impeach.

2.   The writ of *habeas corpus* (the right of a person arrested or imprisoned to be informed of the charges against him) shall not be suspended, "unless, when in cases of rebellion or invasion the public safety may require it." (Article I, section 9, clause 2)

3.   *Bills of attainder* and *ex-post-facto* laws are prohibited. (Article I, section 9, clause 3) Bills of attainder allow legislatures, as opposed to courts, to find persons guilty of treason or felonies; an *ex-post-facto* law subjects people to pun-

135

ishment for acts that, at the time they were committed, were not criminal acts. The great English jurist, Blackstone, believed that prohibiting *ex-post-facto* laws and the right to a writ of *habeas corpus* were the two most fundamental individual rights.

4. The Constitution states that "no title of nobility shall be granted by the United States; and no person holding any office of profit or trust under them, shall, without the consent of the Congress, accept of any present, emolument, office, or title of any kind whatever, from any king, or foreign state." (Article I, section 9, clause 7) We need not insist upon the importance of prohibiting titles of nobility; if such titles were granted, the very foundation of republican government would be undermined.

5. The Constitution guarantees the right to a trial by jury in all criminal cases (except impeachment). (Article 3, section 2, clause 3)

6. Treason is very carefully defined in the Constitution: "treason against the United States shall consist only in levying war against them, or in adhering to their enemies, giving them aid and comfort. No person shall be convicted of treason, unless on the testimony of two witnesses to the same overt act, or on confession in open court. (Article 3, section 3) And the Constitution states in clause 3 of the same section, "the Congress shall have power to declare the punishment of treason; but no attainder of treason shall work corruption of blood, or forfeiture, except during the life of the person attainted." Not only does the Constitution support the essential distinction between political dissent and treason, it does all it can to prevent working a hardship on the traitor's family.

Those who tell you that the New York constitution guarantees individual rights overlook the fact that the state legislature can change the constitution as it sees fit; this means that the state constitution is not adequate security against legislative invasion of the rights of the people. Declarations of rights are intended, after all, to curb the power of the government itself.

Originally, bills of rights were agreements between kings and their subjects concerning the rights of the people. Kings limited their own power, either under pressure or voluntarily, acknowledging that they were not all-powerful. The best example is the Magna Charta, the charter of English liberties which the barons forcibly obtained from King John in 1215. But you must remember that the proposed Constitution has no force unless the people approve it; there is no need to grant them specific rights.

The Preamble of the Constitution is a better recognition of popular rights than all the bills of rights put together. It reads --in part:

> We, THE PEOPLE of the United States, to secure
> the blessings of liberty to ourselves and our
> posterity, do ordain and establish this Consti-
> tution for the United States of America.

The Constitution is concerned with general political interests and rights, not with specific and minute details of every right. The New York constitution is similar in its purpose. It is illogical to praise the state constitution and condemn the national one.

But I go even further than this: a bill of rights is not only unnecessary, it would be dangerous. A bill of rights would, for instance, attempt to limit certain governmental powers which are not even granted! Why state that some things cannot be done when there is no power to do them? Why, for example, should the Constitution state that the freedom of the press shall not be restrained when no power is granted to restrict that freedom? If mention is made of abusing the freedom of the press some clever men might argue that proper regulation of the press is implied. Why not leave well enough alone? This is only one example of how a specific right might be distorted.

I cannot help but make one final remark concerning the liberty of the press. There is not one word about it in the constitution of this state, and in those states where mention is made of it, it amounts to nothing. No government can insure such liberty or deny its existence. Liberty of the press, like all our rights, depends,

137

in the final analysis, upon public opinion and the general spirit
of the government.

Another objection to the Constitution is that the national
government will be so far away from the states and the people that
the latter will be ignorant of what is going on. The same argument
could be advanced by the counties in opposition to state governments. There are ways of knowing what the state governments are up
to, just as there are ways of knowing what is happening in the nation's capitol; we can evaluate the laws that are passed, correspond with our representatives, read newspaper reports, etc. If
this were not so, there would be no division of governmental power
whatsoever in a republican form of government.

Not only will the people be able to take stock of the national
government, the states will act as sentinels or guards; they will
keep a watchful eye over all the branches of the national government. This will be so because the state and national governments
will be rivals for power. Actually, the people will be more fully
informed concerning the conduct of their national representatives
than they are, at present, of the state representatives. Remember,
also, that the people living nearest the national capitol will
keep an eye on the conduct of politicians and will send out alarms,
if necessary, to those who live far away.

There are many curious and extraordinary objections to the
Constitution, but one of the strangest has to do with debts owed
by the states to the United States. Some people have gone so far
as to suggest that the Constitution removes the obligations of the
states to pay their debts. This claim is ridiculous. Common sense
ought to be enough to tell us so, but if it is not, we can turn to
"an established doctrine of political law: states neither lose any
of their rights, nor are discharged from any of their obligations,
by change in the form of the civil government."

The last objection to be examined in this Paper concerns the
expense of the proposed government. When we consider that most
Americans are convinced that Union is vital to their political

happiness, that it cannot be preserved under the present system, that new and broad powers ought to be granted to the national government, the question of added expense seems very superficial. Good government is far too important to allow expense to interfere. Undeniably, there will be some added expense, but there will be some saving as well. For example, Congress is in session all year; much of the business now conducted by Congress, particularly in the area of foreign affairs, will be conducted <u>by the president and the Senate</u>. The fact that Congress will not have to be in session all year will result in a considerable saving of money. Another point to remember is that under the present government the state legislatures are very involved with <u>national</u> matters, with business that goes far beyond the boundaries of the individual states. Under the new government the state legislatures will only have to concern themselves with internal affairs.

The question of increased expense is a weak argument against the adoption of the Constitution.

HAMILTON

To the People of the State of New York:

According to the formal division of the subject of these papers, announced in my first number, there would appear still to remain for discussion two points: "the analogy of the proposed government to your own State constitution," and "the additional security which its adoption will afford to republican government, to liberty, and to property." But these heads have been so fully anticipated and exhausted in the progress of the work, that it would not scarcely be possible to do any thing more than repeat, in a more dilated form, what has been heretofore said, which the advanced stage of the question, and the time already spent upon it, conspire to forbid.

It is remarkable, that the resemblance of the plan of the convention to the act which organizes the government of this State holds, not less with regard to many of the supposed defects, than to the real excellences of the former. Among the pretended defects are the reeligibility of the Executive, the want of a council, the omission of a formal bill of rights, the omission of a provision respecting the liberty of the press. These and several others which have been noted in the course of our inquiries are as much chargeable on the existing constitution of this State, as on the one proposed for the Union; and a man must have slender pretensions to consistency, who can rail at the latter for imperfections which he finds no difficulty in excusing in the former. Nor indeed can there be a better proof of the insincerity and affectation of some of the zealous adversaries of the plan of the convention among us, who profess to be the devoted admirers of the government under which they live, than the fury with which they have attacked that plan, for matters in regard to which our own constitution is equally or perhaps more vulnerable.

The additional securities to republican government, to liberty, and to property, to be derived from the adoption of the plan under consideration, consist chiefly in the restraints which the preservation of the Union will impose on local factions and insurrections, and on the ambition of powerful individuals in single States, who may acquire credit and influence enough, from leaders and favorites, to become the despots of the people; in the diminution of the opportunities to foreign intrigue, which the dissolution of the Confederacy would invite and facilitate; in the prevention of extensive military establishments, which could not fail to grow out of wars between the States in a disunited situation; in the express guaranty of a republican form of government to each; in the absolute and universal exclusion of titles of nobility; and in the precautions against the repetition of those practices on the part of the State governments which have undermined the foundations of property and credit, have planted mutual distrust in the breasts of all classes of citizens, and have occasioned an almost universal prostration of morals.

Thus have I, fellow-citizens, executed the task I had assigned to myself; with what success, your conduct must determine. I trust at least you will admit that I have not failed in the assurance I gave you respecting the spirit with which my endeavors should be conducted. I have addressed muself purely to your judgments, and have studiously avoided those asperities which are too apt to disgrace political disputants of all parties, and which have been not a little provoked by the language and conduct of the opponents of the Constitution. The charge of a conspiracy against the liberties of the people, which has been indiscriminately brought against the advocates of the plan, has something in it too wanton and too malignant, not to excite the indignation of every man who feels in his own bosom a refutation of the calumny. The perpetual changes which have been rung upon the wealthy, the well-born, and the

141

great, have been such as to inspire the disgust of all sensible men. And the unwarrantable concealments and misrepresentations which have been in various ways practised to keep the truth from the public eye, have been of a nature to demand the reprobation of all honest men. It is not impossible that these circumstances may have occasionally betrayed me into intemperances of expression which I did not intend; it is certain that I have frequently felt a struggle between sensibility and moderation; and if the former has in some instances prevailed, it must be my excuse that it has been neither often nor much.

Let us now pause and ask ourselves whether, in the course of these papers, the proposed Constitution has not been satisfactorily vindicated from the aspersions thrown upon it; and whether it has not been shown to be worthy of the public approbation, and necessary to the public safety and prosperity. Every man is bound to answer these questions to himself, according to the best of his conscience and understanding, and to act agreeably to the genuine and sober dictates of his judgment. This is a duty from which nothing can give him a dispensation. 'Tis one that he is called upon, nay, constrained by all the obligations that form the bands of society, to discharge sincerely and honestly. No partial motive, no particular interest, no pride of opinion, no temporary passion or prejudice, will justify to himself, to his country, or to his posterity, an improper election of the part he is to act. Let him beware of an obstinate adherence to party; let him reflect that the object upon which he is to decide is not a particular interest of the community, but the very existence of the nation; and let him remember that a majority of America has already given its sanction to the plan which he is to approve or reject.

I shall not dissemble that I feel an entire confidence in the arguments which recommend the proposed system to your adoption, and that I am unable to discern any real force in those by which it has been opposed. I am persuaded that it is the best which our political situation, habits, and opinions will admit, and superior to any the revolution has produced.

Concessions on the part of the friends of the plan, that it has not a claim to absolute perfection, have afforded matter of no small triumph to its enemies. "Why," say they, "should we adopt an imperfect thing? Why not amend it and make it perfect before it is irrevocably established?" This may be plausible enough, but it is only plausible. In the first place I remark, that the extent of these concessions has been greatly exaggerated. They have been stated as amounting to an admission that the plan is radically defective, and that without material alterations the rights and the interests of the community cannot be safely confided to it. This, as far as I have understood the meaning of those who make the concessions, is an entire perversion of their sense. No advocate of the measure can be found, who will not declare as his sentiment, that the system, though it may not be perfect in every part, is, upon the whole, a good one; is the best that the present views and circumstances of the country will permit; and is such an one as promises every species of security which a reasonable people can desire.

I answer in the next place, that I should esteem it the extreme of imprudence to prolong the precarious state of our national affairs, and to expose the Union to the jeopardy of successive experiments, in the chimerical pursuit of a perfect plan. I never expect to see a perfect work from imperfect man. The result of the deliberations of all collective bodies must necessarily be a compound, as well of the errors and prejudices, as of the good sense and wisdom, of the individuals of whom they are composed. The compacts which are to embrace thirteen distinct States in a common bond of amity and union, must as necessarily be a compromise of as many dissimilar interests and inclinations. How can perfection spring from such materials?

The reasons assigned in an excellent little pamphlet lately published in this city,* are unanswerable to show the utter improb-
_____
* Entitled "An Address to the People of the State of New York."
--PUBLIUS

ability of assembling a new convention, under circumstances in any degree so favorable to a happy issue, as those in which the late convention met, deliberated, and concluded. I will not repeat the arguments there used, as I presume the production itself has had an extensive circulation. It is certainly well worthy of the perusal of every friend to his country. There is, however, one point of light in which the subject of amendments still remains to be considered, and in which it has not yet been exhibited to public view. I cannot resolve to conclude without first taking a survey of it in this aspect.

It appears to me susceptible of absolute demonstration, that it will be far more easy to obtain subsequent than previous amendments to the Constitution. The moment an alteration is made in the present plan, it becomes, to the purpose of adoption, a new one, and must undergo a new decision of each State. To its complete establishment throughout the Union, it will therefore require the concurrence of thirteen States. If, on the contrary, the Constitution proposed should once be ratified by all the States as it stands, alterations in it may at any time be effected by nine States. Here, then, the chances are as thirteen to nine* in favor of subsequent amendment, rather than of the original adoption of an entire system.

This is not all. Every Constitution for the United States must inevitably consist of a great variety of particulars, in which thirteen independent States are to be accommodated in their interests or opinions of interest. We may of course expect to see, in any body of men charged with its original formation, very different combinations of the parts upon different points. Many of those who form a majority on one question, may become the minority on a second, and an association dissimilar to either may constitute the majority on a third. Hence the necessity of moulding and arranging

---

* It may rather be said TEN, for though two thirds may set on foot the measure, three fourths must ratify. --PUBLIUS

144

all the particulars which are to compose the whole, in such a manner as to satisfy all the parties to the compact; and hence, also,
an immense multiplication of difficulties and casualties in obtaining the collective assent to a final act. The degree of that multiplication must evidently be in a ratio to the number of particulars and the number of parties.

But every amendment to the Constitution, if once established,
would be a single proposition, and might be brought forward singly.
There would then be no necessity for management or compromise, in
relation to any other point--no giving nor taking. The will of the
requisite number would at once bring the matter to a decisive issue. And consequently, whenever nine, or rather ten States, were
united in the desire of a particular amendment that amendment must
infallibly take place. There can, therefore, be no comparison between the facility of affecting an amendment, and that of establishing in the first instance a complete Constitution.

In opposition to the probability of subsequent amendments, it
has been urged that the persons delegated to the administration of
the national government will always be disinclined to yield up any
portion of the authority of which they were once possessed. For
my own part, I acknowledge a thorough conviction that any amendments which may, upon mature consideration, be thought useful, will
be applicable to the organization of the government, not to the
mass of its powers; and on this account alone, I think there is no
weight in the observation just stated. I also think there is little weight in it on another account. The intrinsic difficulty of
governing thirteen States at any rate, independent of calculations
upon an ordinary degree of public spirit and integrity, will, in
my opinion, constantly impose on the national rulers the necessity
of a spirit of accommodation to the reasonable expectations of
their constituents. But there is yet a further consideration,
which proves beyond the possibility of a doubt, that the observation is futile. It is this, that the national rulers, whenever
nine States concur, will have no option upon the subject. By the

145

fifth article of the plan, the Congress will be obliged "on the application of the legislatures of two thirds of the States (which at present amount to nine), to call a convention for proposing amendments, which shall be valid, to all intents and purposes, as part of the Constitution, when ratified by the legislatures of three fourths of the States, or by conventions in three fourths thereof." The words of this article are peremptory. The Congress "shall call a convention." Nothing in this particular is left to the discretion of that body. And of consequence, all the declamation about the disinclination to a change vanishes in air. Nor however difficult it may be supposed to unite two thirds or three fourths of the State legislatures, in amendments which may affect local interests, can there be any room to apprehend any such difficulty in a union on points which are merely relative to the general liberty or security of the people. We may safely rely on the disposition of the State legislatures to erect barriers against the encroachments of the national authority.

If the foregoing argument is a fallacy, certain it is that I am myself deceived by it, for it is, in my conception, one of those rare instances in which a political truth can be brought to the test of a mathematical demonstration. Those who see the matter in the same light with me, however zealous they may be for amendments, must agree in the propriety of a previous adoption, as the most direct road to their own object.

The zeal for attempts to amend, prior to the establishment of the Constitution, must abate in every man who is ready to accede to the truth of the following observations of a writer equally solid and ingenious: "To balance a large state or society (says he), whether monarchical or republican, on general laws, is a work of so great difficulty, that no human genius, however comprehensive, is able, by the mere dint of reason and reflection, to effect it. The judgments of many must unite in the work; experience must guide their labor; time must bring it to perfection, and the feeling of inconveniences must correct the mistakes which they *inevi-*

146

tably fall into in their first trials and experiments."* These judicious reflections contain a lesson of moderation to all the sincere lovers of the Union, and ought to put them upon their guard against hazarding anarchy, civil war, a perpetual alienation of the States from each other, and perhaps the military despotism of a victorious demagogue, in the pursuit of what they are not likely to obtain, but from time and experience. It may be in me a defect of political fortitude, but I acknowledge that I cannot entertain an equal tranquility with those who affect to treat the dangers of a longer continuance in our present situation as imaginary. A nation, without a national government, is, in my view, an awful spectacle. The establishment of a Constitution, in time of profound peace, by the voluntary consent of a whole people, is a prodigy, to the completion of which I look forward with trembling anxiety. I can reconcile it to no rules of prudence to let go the hold we now have, in so arduous an enterprise, upon seven out of the thirteen States, and after having passed over so considerable a part of the ground, to recommence the course. I dread the more the consequences of new attempts, because I know that powerful individuals, in this and in other States, are enemies to a general national government in every possible shape.

PUBLIUS

---

* Hume's "Essays," vol. i., page 128: "The Rise of Arts and Sciences."   --PUBLIUS

SELECTED READINGS AND COMMENTS

Max Farrand, (ed.), *The Records of the Federal Convention of 1787*
(New Haven: Yale University Press, 1937, 4 vols.), is indispensable
to the study of the Convention. These volumes contain Madison's
Notes as well as other valuable source material. (These volumes
are now available in paperback.) Alfred H. Kelly & Winfred A.
Harbison's *The American Constitution* (New York, 1948) is a particularly valuable book for a comprehensive discussion of the Convention and ratification (see especially, chapters 4, 5, 6, and 7).
A. C. McLaughlin, *The Confederation and the Constitution* (New York,
1905) contrasts the government under the Articles with the government established by the Constitution. Max Farrand, *The Framing of
the Constitution of the United States* (New Haven, 1913) is primari-
ly concerned with constitutional issues and personalities of the
framers. His book, *The Fathers of the Constitution* (New Haven,
1913), still stands as an excellent summary of the Convention.
Charles A. Beard's, *An Economic Interpretation of the Constitution
of the United States* (New York, 1913) is perhaps the most controversial work concerning the motives of the framers and cannot be
overlooked in any serious study of the Constitution. Many scholars
have attacked Beard's thesis. See especially: A. C. McLaughlin,
A Constitutional History of the United States (New York, 1935);
Forrest McDonald, *We The People: The Economic Origins of the Constitution* (Chicago, 1963), and Robert E. Brown, *Charles Beard and
the Constitution* (Princeton, N.J., 1956). Adrienne Koch's introduction to the 1966 edition (Athens, Ohio) of *Notes of Debates in
the Federal Convention of 1787 Reported by James Madison* is a per-
ceptive introduction to the study of the Constitution and the framers. See also her superb study, *Jefferson & Madison: The Great
Collaboration* (New York, 1966). Almost all the important literature concerning the ratification debate can be found in Paul L.

Ford (ed.), *Essays on the Constitution* (New York, 1892) (reprinted 1970). An excellent and recent volume of selected documents is John D. Lewis, (ed.) *Anti-Federalists versus Federalists* (San Francisco, 1967). Every student of American government should consult Alexis de Tocqueville's *Democracy in America* (first published in English in 1835 and available today in many editions). I particularly recommend the first three chapters of Daniel Boorstin's, *The Genius of American Politics* (Chicago, 1953); Hannah Arendt's *Crises of the Republic* (New York, 1969), and Hans J. Morgenthau's *The Purpose of American Politics* (New York, 1964). I also highly recommend Arthur M. Schlesinger's *The Imperial Presidency* (Boston: 1973). This is obviously an abridged list, and I have not re-listed many of the books and articles referred to under *Notes*. The latter are, however, valuable to a study of the Convention and *The Federalist*, particularly Benjamin F. Wright's Introduction to the Harvard University Press edition of *The Federalist* (1961).

APPENDIX I

RESOLUTION TRANSMITTING THE CONSTITUTION TO CONGRESS

IN CONVENTION

Monday, September 17, 1787

PRESENT, *The States of New-Hampshire, Massachusetts, Connecticut, Mr. Hamilton from New-York, New Jersey, Pennsylvania, Delaware, Maryland, Virginia, North Carolina, South Carolina, and Georgia.*

Resolved, That the (following) Constitution be laid before the United States in Congress assembled, and that it is the opinion of this convention, that it should afterwards be submitted to a convention of delegates, chosen in each State by the people thereof, under the recommendation of its legislature, for their assent and ratification; and that each convention assenting to, and ratifying the same should give notice thereof to the United States in Congress assembled.

Resolved, That it is the opinion of this convention, that as soon as the conventions of nine States shall have ratified this Constitution, the United States in Congress assembled should fix a day on which electors should be appointed by the States which shall have ratified the same, and a day on which the electors should assemble to vote for the President, and the time and place for commencing proceedings under this Constitution; that after such publication the electors should be appointed, and the senators and representatives elected; that the electors should meet on the day fixed for the election of the President, and should transmit their votes certified, signed, sealed, and directed, as the Constitution requires, to the secretary of the United States in Congress assembled; that the senators and representatives should convene at the time and place assigned; that the senators should appoint a president of the Senate, for the sole purpose of receiving, opening, and counting the votes for President; and that after he shall be chosen, the Congress, together with the President, should without delay proceed to execute this Constitution.

By the unanimous order of the convention.

GEORGE WASHINGTON, *President.*

William Jackson, *Secretary.**

---

* Max Farrand, *Records of the Federal Convention,* Volume II, pp. 665-666.

WASHINGTON'S LETTER OF TRANSMITTAL

IN CONVENTION

September 17, 1787

SIR,

We have now the honor to submit to the consideration of the United States in Congress assembled, that Constitution which has appeared to us the most advisable.

The friends of our country have long seen and desired, that the power of making war, peace, and treaties, of levying money and regulating commerce, and the correspondent executive and judicial authorities should be fully and effectually vested in the general government of the Union: but the impropriety of delegating such extensive trust to one body of men is evident--Hence results the necessity of a different organization.

It is obviously impracticable in the federal government of these States, to secure all rights of independent sovereignty to each, and yet provide for the interest and safety of all--Individuals entering into society, must give up a share of liberty to preserve the rest. The magnitude of the sacrifice must depend as well on situation and circumstances as on the object to be obtained. It is at all times difficult to draw with precision the line between those rights which must be surrendered, and those which may be reserved; and on the present occasion this difficulty was increased by a difference among the several States as to their situation, extent, habits, and particular interests.

In all our deliberations on this subject we kept steadily in our view, that which appears to us the greatest interest of every true American, the consolidation of our Union, in which is involved our prosperity, felicity, safety, perhaps our national existence. This important consideration, seriously and deeply impressed on our minds, led each State in the Convention to be less rigid on points of inferior magnitude, than might have been otherwise expected; and thus the Constitution, which we now present, is the result of a spirit of amity, and of that mutual deference and concession which the peculiarity of our political situation rendered indispensable.

That it will meet the full and entire approbation of every State is not perhaps to be expected; but each will doubtless consider, that had her interest alone been consulted, the consequences might have been particularly disagreeable or injurious to others; that it is liable to as few exceptions as could reasonably have been expected, we hope and believe; that it may promote the lasting wel-

fare of that country so dear to us all, and secure her freedom
and happiness, is our most ardent wish.

> With great respect,
>   We have the honor to be
>   SIR,
>   Your Excellency's most
>   Obedient and Humble Servants,
>   GEORGE WASHINGTON, President

By Unanimous Order of the Convention
        HIS EXCELLENCY
    THE PRESIDENT OF CONGRESS*

---

    *Max Farrand, *Records of the Federal Convention,* Volume II,
p. 666.

THE CONSTITUTION OF THE UNITED STATES

As Agreed Upon

BY THE CONVENTION

SEPTEMBER 17, 1787

WE, *the People of the United States, in order to form a more per-*
fect Union, establish Justice, insure domestic Tranquility, provide
for the common Defence, promote the general Welfare, and secure the
Blessings of Liberty to ourselves and our posterity, do ordain and
establish this CONSTITUTION for the United States of America.

ARTICLE I

SECTION 1. All legislative powers herein granted shall be vested in
a Congress of the United States which shall consist of a Senate and
House of Representatives.

SECT. 2. The House of Representatives shall be composed of members chosen every second year by the people of the several States,
and the electors in each State shall have the qualifications requisite for electors of the most numerous branch of the State legislature.

No person shall be a representative who shall not have attained
to the age of twenty-five years, and been seven years a citizen of
the United States, and who shall not, when elected, be an inhabitant of that State in which he shall be chosen.

Representatives and direct taxes shall be apportioned among the
several States which may be included within this Union, according
to their respective numbers, which shall be determined by adding
to the whole number of free persons, including those bound to service for a term of years, and excluding Indians not taxed, three
fifths of all other persons. The actual enumeration shall be made
within three years after the first meeting of the Congress of the
United States, and within every subsequent term of ten years, in
such manner as they shall by law direct. The number of representatives shall not exceed one for every thirty thousand but each
State shall have at least one representative; and until such enumeration shall be made, the State of New Hampshire shall be entitled to choose three, Massachusetts eight, Rhode Island and Providence Plantations one, Connecticut five, New York six, New Jersey
four, Pennsylvania eight, Delaware one, Maryland six, Virginia ten,
North Carolina five, South Carolina five, and Georgia three.

When vacancies happen in the representation from any State, the
executive authority thereof shall issue writs of election to fill
such vacancies.

When vacancies happen in the representation from any State, the executive authority thereof shall issue writs of election to fill such vacancies.

The house of representatives shall choose their Speaker and other officers; and shall have the sole power of impeachment.

SECT. 3. The Senate of the United States shall be composed of two senators from each State, chosen by the legislature thereof, for six years; and each senator shall have one vote.

Immediately after they shall be assembled in consequence of the first election, they shall be divided as equally as may be into three classes. The seats of the senators of the first class shall be vacated at the expiration of the second year, the second class at the expiration of the fourth year and the third class at the expiration of the sixth year, so that one third may be chosen every second year; and if vacancies happen, by resignation or otherwise, during the recess of the legislature of any State, the Executive thereof may make temporary appointments until the next meeting of the legislature, which shall then fill such vacancies.

No person shall be a senator who shall not have attained to the age of thirty years, and been nine years a citizen of the United States, and who shall not, when elected, be an inhabitant of that State for which he shall be chosen.

The Vice-President of the United States shall be president of the Senate, but shall have no vote, unless they be equally divided.

The Senate shall choose their other officers, and also a president *pro tempore*, in the absence of the Vice-President, or when he shall exercise the office of President of the United States.

The Senate shall have the sole power to try all impeachments. When sitting for that purpose they shall be on oath or affirmation. When the President of the United States is tried, the Chief-Justice shall preside. And no person shall be convicted without the concurrence of two thirds of the members present.

Judgment in cases of impeachment shall not extend further than to removal from office, and disqualification to hold and enjoy any office of honor, trust, or profit under the United States; but the party convicted shall, nevertheless, be liable and subject to indictment, trial, judgment, and punishment, according to law.

SECT. 4. The times, places, and manner of holding elections for senators and representatives shall be prescribed in each State by the legislature thereof; but the Congress may at any time by law make or alter such regulations, except as to the places of choosing senators.

The Congress shall assemble at least once in every year, and such meeting shall be on the first Monday in December, unless they shall by law appoint a different day.

SECT. 5. Each house shall be the judge of the elections, returns, and qualifications of its own members; and a majority of each shall constitute a quorum to do business; but a smaller number may adjourn from day to day, and may be authorized to compel the attendance of absent members, in such manner, and under such penalties, as each house may provide.

Each house may determine the rules of its proceedings, punish its members for disorderly behavior, and, with the concurrence of two thirds, expel a member.

Each house shall keep a journal of its proceedings, and from time to time publish the same excepting such parts as may in their judgment require secrecy; and the yeas and nays of the members of either house on any question, shall, at the desire of one fifth of those present, be entered on the journal.

Neither house, during the session of Congress, shall, without the consent of the other, adjourn for more than three days, nor to any other place than that in which the two houses shall be sitting.

SECT. 6. The senators and representatives shall receive a compensation for their services, to be ascertained by law, and paid out of the treasury of the United States. They shall, in all cases, except treason, felony, and breach of the peace, be privileged from arrest during their attendance at the session of their respective houses, and in going to and returning from the same; and for any speech or debate in either house, they shall not be questioned in any other place.

No senator or representative shall, during the time for which he was elected, be appointed to any civil office under the authority of the United States, which shall have been created, or the emoluments whereof shall have been increased, during such time; and no person holding any office under the United States, shall be a member of either house during his continuance in office.

SECT. 7. All bills for raising revenue shall originate in the House of Representatives; but the Senate may propose or concur with amendments as on other bills.

Every bill which shall have passed the House of Representatives and the Senate shall, before it becomes a law, be presented to the President of the United States; if he approve, he shall sign it; but if not, he shall return it, with his objections, to that house in which it shall have originated, who shall enter the objections at large on their journal, and proceed to reconsider it. If after such reconsideration two thirds of that house shall agree to pass the bill, it shall be sent, together with the objections, to the other house, by which it shall likewise be reconsidered, and if approved by two thirds of that house, it shall become a law. But in all such cases the votes of both houses shall be determined by yeas and nays, and the names of the persons voting for and against the bill shall be entered on the journal of each house respectively. If any bill shall not be returned by the President within ten days (Sundays excepted) after it shall have been presented to him, the same shall be a law, in like manner as if he had signed it, unless the Congress by their adjournment prevent its return, in which case it shall not be a law.

Every order, resolution, or vote, to which the concurrence of the Senate and the House of Representatives may be necessary (except on a question of adjournment), shall be presented to the President of the United States; and before the same shall take effect, shall be approved by him, or, being disapproved by him, shall be repassed by two thirds of the Senate and House of Representatives, according to the rules and limitations prescribed in the case of a bill.

SECT. 8. The Congress shall have power--

To lay and collect taxes, duties, imposts, and excises; to pay the debts and provide for the common defence and general welfare of the United States; but all duties, imposts, and excises, shall be uniform throughout the United States;

To borrow money on the credit of the United States;

To regulate commerce with foreign nations, and among the several States, and with the Indian tribes;

To establish a uniform rule of naturalization, and uniform laws on the subject of backruptcies throughout the United States;

To coin money, regulate the value thereof, and of foreign coin, and fix the standard of weights and measures;

To provide for the punishment of counterfeiting the securities and current coin of the United States;

To establish post-offices and post-roads;

To promote the progress of science and useful arts, by securing for limited times to authors and inventors the exclusive right to their respective writings and discoveries;

To constitute tribunals inferior to the Supreme Court;

To define and punish piracies and felonies committed on the high seas, and offences against the law of nations;

To declare war, grant letters of marque and reprisal, and make rules concerning captures on land and water;

To raise and support armies, but no appropriation of money to that use shall be for a longer term than two years;

To provide and maintain a navy;

To make rules for the government and regulation of the land and naval forces;

To provide for calling forth the militia to execute the laws of the Union, suppress insurrections, and repel invasions;

To provide for organizing, arming, and disciplining the militia, and for governing such parts of them as may be employed in the service of the United States, reserving to the States respectively, the appointment of the officers, and the authority of training the militia according to the discipline prescribed by Congress;

To exercise exclusive legislation in all cases whatsoever, over such district (not exceeding ten miles square) as may, by cession of particular States, and the acceptance of Congress, become the seat of the government of the United States, and to exercise like authority over all places purchased by the consent of the legislature of the State in which the same shall be, for the erection of forts, magazines, arsenals, dock-yards, and other needful buildings; And

To make all laws which shall be necessary and proper for carrying into execution the foregoing powers, and all other powers vested by this Constitution in the government of the United States, or in any department or officer thereof.

SECT. 9. The migration or importation of such persons as any of the States now existing shall think proper to admit, shall not be prohibited by the Congress prior to the year one thousand eight hundred and eight, but a tax or duty may be imposed on such importation, not exceeding ten dollars for each person.

The privilege of the writ of *habeas corpus* shall not be suspended, unless when in cases of rebellion or invasion the public safety may require it.

No bill of attainder or *ex-post-facto* law shall be passed.

No capitation, or other direct, tax shall be laid, unless in proportion to the *census* or enumeration herein before directed to be taken.

No tax or duty shall be laid on articles exported from any State. No preference shall be given by any regulation of commerce or revenue to the ports of one State over those of another; nor shall vessels bound to, or from, one State, be obliged to enter, clear, or pay duties in another.

No money shall be drawn from the treasury, but in consequence of appropriations made by law; and a regular statement and account of the receipts and expenditures of all public money shall be published from time to time.

No title of nobility shall be granted by the United States; And no person holding any office of profit or trust under them, shall, without the consent of the Congress, accept of any present, emolument, office, or title, of any kind whatever, from any king, prince, or foreign state.

SECT. 10. No state shall enter into any treaty, alliance, or confederation; grant letters of marque and reprisal; coin money; emit bills of credit; make any thing but gold and silver coin a tender in payment of debts; pass any bill of attainder, *ex-post-facto* law, or law impairing the obligation of contracts; or grant any title of nobility.

No State shall, without the consent of the Congress, lay any imposts or duties on imports or exports, except what may be absolutely necessary for executing its inspection laws; and the net proceeds of all duties and imposts, laid by any State on imports or exports, shall be for the use of the treasury of the United States; and all such laws shall be subject to the revision and control of the Congress. No State shall, without the consent of Congress, lay any duties of tonnage, keep troops, or ships of war, in time of peace, enter into any agreement or compact with another state, or with a foreign power, or engage in war, unless actually invaded, or in such imminent danger as will not admit of delay.

ARTICLE II

SECTION 1. The executive power shall be vested in a President of the United States of America. He shall hold his office during the term of four years, and, together with the Vice-President, chosen for the same term, be elected as follows:

Each State shall appoint, in such manner as the legislature thereof may direct, a number of electors, equal to the whole number of senators and representatives to which the State may be entitled in the Congress; but no senator or representative, or person holding an office of trust or profit under the United States, shall be appointed an elector.

The electors shall meet in their respective States, and vote by ballot for two persons, of whom one at least shall not be an inhabitant of the same State with themselves. And they shall make a list of all the persons voted for, and of the number of votes for each; which list they shall sign and certify, and transmit sealed to the seat of the government of the United States, directed to the president of the Senate. The president of the Senate shall, in the presence of the Senate and House of Representatives, open all the certificates, and the votes shall then be counted. The person having the greatest number of votes shall be the President, if such number be a majority of the whole number of electors appointed; and if there be more than one who have such majority, and have an equal number of votes, then the House of Representatives shall immediately choose by ballot one of them for President; and if no person have a majority, then from the five highest on the list the said House shall in like manner choose the President. But in choosing the President, the votes shall be taken by States, the representation from each State having one vote; a quorum for this purpose shall consist of a member or members from two thirds of the States, and a majority of all the States shall be necessary to a choice. In every case, after the choice of the President, the person having the greatest number of votes of the electors shall be the Vice-President. But if there should remain two or more who have equal votes, the Senate shall choose from them by ballot the Vice-President.

The Congress may determine the time of choosing the electors, and the day on which they shall give their votes; which day shall be the same throughout the United States.

No person except a natural-born citizen, or a citizen of the United States, at the time of the adoption of this Constitution, shall be eligible to the office of President; neither shall any person be eligible to that office who shall not have attained to the age of thirty-five years, and been fourteen years a resident within the United States.

In case of removal of the President from office, or of his death, resignation, or inability to discharge the powers and duties of the said office, the same shall devolve on the Vice-President, and the Congress may by law provide for the case of removal, death, resignation, or inability, both of the President and Vice-President, declaring what officer shall then act as President, and such office shall act accordingly, until the disability be removed, or a President shall be elected.

The President shall, at stated times, receive for his services a compensation, which shall neither be increased nor diminished during the period for which he shall have been elected, and he shall not receive within that period any other emolument from the United States, or any of them.

Before he enter on the execution of his office, he shall take the following oath or affirmation:

"I do solemnly swear (or affirm) that I will faithfully execute the office of President of the United States, and will, to the best of my ability, preserve, protect, and defend the Constitution of the United States."

SECT. 2. The President shall be commander-in-chief of the army and navy of the United States; and of the militia of the several States, when called into the actual service of the United States; he may require the opinion, in writing, of the principal officer in each of the executive departments, upon any subject relating to the duties of their respective offices, and he shall have power to grant reprieves and pardons for offences against the United States, except in cases of impeachment.

He shall have power, by and with the advice and consent of the Senate, to make treaties, provided two thirds of the senators present concur; and he shall nominate, and, by and with the advice and consent of the Senate, shall appoint ambassadors, other public ministers and consuls, judges of the Supreme Court, and all other officers of the United States, whose appointments are not herein otherwise provided for, and which shall be established by law. But the Congress may by law vest the appointment of such inferior officers, as they think proper, in the President alone, in the courts of law, or in the heads of departments.

The President shall have power to fill up all vacancies that may happen during the recess of the Senate, by granting commissions which shall expire at the end of their next session.

SECT. 3. He shall from time to time give to the Congress information of the state of the Union, and recommend to their consideration such measures as he shall judge necessary and expedient; he may, on extraordinary occasions, convene both houses, or either of them, and in case of disagreement between them, with respect to the time of adjournment, he may adjourn them to such time as he shall think proper; he shall receive ambassadors and other public ministers; he shall take care that the laws be faithfully executed, and shall commission all the officers of the United States.

SECT. 4. The President, Vice-President, and all civil officers of the United States shall be removed from office on impeachment for, and conviction of, treason, bribery, or other high crimes and misdemeanors.

ARTICLE III

SECTION 1. The judicial power of the United States shall be vested in one Supreme Court, and in such inferior courts as the Congress may from time to time ordain and establish. The judges, both of the supreme and inferior courts, shall hold their offices during good behavior, and shall, at stated times, receive for their services a compensation, which shall not be diminished during their continuance in office.

SECT. 2. The judicial power shall extend to all cases in law and equity arising under this Constitution, the laws of the United States, and treaties made, or which shall be made, under their authority; to all cases affecting ambassadors, other public ministers and consuls; to all cases of admiralty and maritime jurisdiction; to controversies to which the United States shall be a party; to controversies between two or more States; between a State and citizen of another State; between citizens of different States; between citizens of the same State claiming lands under grants of different States; and between a State, or the citizens thereof, and foreign states, citizens, or subjects.

In all cases affecting ambassadors, other public ministers and consuls, and those in which a State shall be party, the Supreme Court shall have original jurisdiction. In all the other cases before mentioned, the Supreme Court shall have appellate jurisdiction, both as to law and fact, with such exceptions, and under such regulations, as the Congress shall make.

The trial of all crimes, except in cases of impeachment, shall be by jury; and such trial shall be held in the State where the said crimes shall have been committed; but when not committed within any State, the trial shall be at such place or places as the Congress may by law have directed.

SECT. 3. Treason against the United States shall consist only in levying war against them, or in adhering to their enemies, giving them aid and comfort. No person shall be convicted of treason unless on the testimony of two witnesses to the same overt act, or on confession in open court.

The Congress shall have power to declare the punishment of treason, but no attainder of treason shall work corruption of blood, or forfeiture, except during the life of the person attainted.

ARTICLE IV

SECTION 1. Full faith and credit shall be given in each State to the public acts, records, and judicial proceedings of every other State. And the Congress may by general laws prescribe the manner in which such acts, records, and proceedings shall be proved, and the effect thereof.

SECT. 2. The citizens of each State shall be entitled to all privileges and immunities of citizens in the several States.

A person charged in any State with treason, felony, or other crime, who shall flee from justice, and be found in another State, shall, on demand of the executive authority of the State from which he fled, be delivered up, to be removed to the State having jurisdiction of the crime.

No person held to service or labor in one State, under the laws thereof, escaping into another, shall, in consequence of any law or regulation therein, be discharged from such service or labor, but shall be delivered up on claim of the party to whom such service or labor may be due.

SECT. 3. New States may be admitted by the Congress into this Union; but no new State shall be formed or erected within the jurisdiction of any other State, nor any State be formed by the junction of two or more States, or parts of States, without the consent of the legislatures of the States concerned, as well as of the Congress.

The Congress shall have power to dispose of and make all needful rules and regulations respecting the territory or other property belonging to the United States; and nothing in this Constitution shall be so construed as to prejudice any claims of the United States, or of any particular State.

SECT. 4. The United States shall guarantee to every State in this Union a republican form of government, and shall protect each of them against invasion, and on application of the legislature, or of the Executive (when the legislature cannot be convened), against domestic violence.

ARTICLE V

The Congress, whenever two thirds of both houses shall deem it necessary, shall propose amendments to this Constitution, or, on the application of the legislatures of two thirds of the several States, shall call a convention for proposing amendments, which, in either case, shall be valid to all intents and purposes, as part of this Constitution, when ratified by the legislatures of three fourths of the several States, or by conventions in three fourths thereof, as the one or the other mode of ratification may be proposed by the Congress: Provided, that no amendment which may be made prior to the year one thousand eight hundred and eight, shall in any manner affect the first and fourth clauses in the ninth section of the first article; and that no State, without its consent, shall be deprived of its equal suffrage in the Senate.

ARTICLE VI

All debts contracted and engagements entered into, before the adoption of this Constitution, shall be as valid against the United States under this Constitution, as under the Confederation.

This Constitution, and the laws of the United States which shall be made in pursuance thereof; and all treaties made, or which shall be made, under the authority of the United States, shall be the supreme law of the land; and the judges in every State shall be bound thereby, any thing in the Constitution or laws of any State to the contrary notwithstanding.

The senators and representatives before mentioned, and the members of the several State legislatures, and all executive and judicial officers, both of the United States and of the several States, shall be bound by oath or affirmation to support this Constitution; but no religious test shall ever be required as a qualification to any office or public trust under the United States.

ARTICLE VII

The ratification of the conventions of nine States shall be suffi-

cient for the establishment of this Constitution between the
States to ratifying the same.

DONE in convention, by the unanimous consent of the States present,
the seventeeth day of September, in the year of our Lord one
thousand seven hundred and eighty-seven, and of the independence
of the United States of America the twelfth. In witness whereof,
we have hereunto subscribed our names.

GEORGE WASHINGTON, *President, and Deputy from Virginia.*

NEW-HAMPSHIRE . . . . .
John Langdon,
Nicholas Gilman.

MASSACHUSETTS . . . . .
Nathaniel Gorham,
Rufus King.

CONNECTICUT . . . . . .
William Samuel Johnson,
Roger Sherman.

NEW YORK . . . . Alexander Hamilton.

NEW JERSEY . . . . . .
William Livingston,
David Brearley,
William Paterson,
Jonathan Dayton.

PENNSYLVANIA . . . . .
Benjamin Franklin
Thomas Mifflin,
Robert Morris,
George Clymer,
Thomas Fitzsimons,
Jared Ingersoll,
James Wilson,
Gouverneur Morris.

DELAWARE . . . .
George Read,
Gunning Bedford, Junior,
John Dickinson,
Richard Bassett,
Jacob Broom.

MARYLAND . . . .
James M'Henry,
Daniel Jenifer, of St. Thomas,
Daniel Carroll.

VIRGINIA . . . .
John Blair,
James Madison, Junior.

NORTH CAROLINA . . . .
William Blount,
Richard Dobbs Spaight,
Hugh Williamson.

SOUTH CAROLINA . . . .
John Rutledge,
Charles Cotesworth Pinckney,
Charles Pinckney,
Pierce Butler.

GEORGIA . . . .
William Few,
Abraham Baldwin.

Attest.   WILLIAM JACKSON, *Secretary.*

162

BILL OF RIGHTS

ARTICLE THE FIRST

Congress shall make no law respecting the establishment of religion, or prohibiting the free exercise thereof; or abridging the freedom of speech, or of the press; or the right of the people peaceably to assemble, and to petition the government for a redress of grievances.

ARTICLE THE SECOND

A well regulated militia being necessary to the security of a free State, the right of the people to keep and bear arms shall not be infringed.

ARTICLE THE THIRD

No soldier shall, in time of peace, be quartered in any house without the consent of the owner; nor in time of war, but in the manner prescribed by law.

ARTICLE THE FOURTH

The right of the people to be secure in their persons, houses, papers, and effects, against unreasonable searches and seizures, shall not be violated, and no warrants shall issue, but upon probable cause, supported by oath or affirmation, and particularly describing the place to be searched, and the persons or things to be seized.

ARTICLE THE FIFTH

No person shall be held to answer for a capital or otherwise infamous crime, unless on a presentment or indictment of a grand jury, except in cases arising in the land or naval forces, or in the militia when in actual service in time of war or public danger; not shall any person be subject for the same offence to be twice put in jeopardy of life or limb; nor shall be compelled in any criminal case to be witness against himself; nor be deprived of life, liberty, or property, without due process of law; nor shall private property be taken for public use without just compensation.

ARTICLE THE SIXTH

In all criminal prosecutions the accused shall enjoy the right of a speedy and public trial, by an impartial jury of the State and district wherein the crime shall have been committed, which district shall have been previously ascertained by law, and to be informed of the nature and cause of the accusation; to be confronted with the witnesses against him; to have compulsory process for obtaining witnesses in his favor, and to have the assistance of counsel for his defence.

ARTICLE THE SEVENTH

In suits at common law, where the value in controversy shall exceed twenty dollars, the right of trial by jury shall be preserved; and no fact tried by a jury, shall be otherwise reexamined in any court of the United States than according to the rules of the common law.

ARTICLE THE EIGHTH

Excessive bail shall not be required, nor excessive fines imposed, nor cruel and unusual punishments inflicted.

ARTICLE THE NINTH

The enumeration in the Constitution of certain rights, shall not be construed to deny or disparage others retained by the people.

ARTICLE THE TENTH

The powers not delegated to the United States by the Constitution or prohibited by it to the States, are reserved to the States respectively, or to the people.

AMENDMENTS

AMENDMENT 11

The judicial power of the United States shall not be construed to extend to any suit in law or equity, commenced or prosecuted against one of the United States by citizens of another State, or by citizens or subjects of any foreign State.

AMENDMENT 12

The electors shall meet in their respective States, and vote by ballot for President and Vice-President, one of whom, at least shall not be an inhabitant of the same State with themselves; they shall name in their ballots the person voted for as President, and in distinct ballots the person voted for as Vice-President; and they shall make distinct lists of all persons voted for as President, and of all persons voted for as Vice-President, and of the number of votes for each, which lists they shall sign and certify, and transmit sealed to the seat of government of the United States, directed to the President of the Senate; the president of the Senate shall, in the presence of the Senate and the House of Representatives, open all the certificates, and the votes shall then be counted; the person having the greatest number of votes for President, shall be the President, if such number be a majority of the whole number of electors appointed; and if no person have such majority, then from the persons having the highest numbers, not exceeding three, on the list of those voted for as President, the House of Representatives shall choose immediately, by ballot, the President. But in choosing the President, the votes shall be taken by States, the representation from each State having one vote; a quorum for this purpose shall consist of a member or members from two thirds of the States, and a majority of all the States shall be necessary to a choice. And if the House of Representatives shall not choose a President whenever the right of choice shall devolve upon them, before the fourth day of March next following, then the Vice-President shall act as President as in the case of the death or other constitutional disability of the President.

The person having the greatest number of votes as Vice-President, shall be the Vice-President, if such number be a majority of the whole number of electors appointed; and if no person have a majority, then from the two highest numbers on the list, the Senate shall choose the Vice-President; a quorum for the purpose shall consist of two thirds of the whole number of senators, and a majority of the whole number shall be necessary to a choice.

But no person constitutionally ineligible to the office of President shall be eligible to that of Vice-President of the United States.

The following amendment was ratified by Alabama, December 2,

1865, which filled the requisite complement of ratifying States, and was certified by the Secretary of State to have become valid as a part of the Constitution of the United States, December 18, 1865.

AMENDMENT 13

SECT. 1. Neither slavery nor involuntary servitude, except as a punishment for crime, whereof the party shall have been duly convicted, shall exist within the United States, or any place subject to their jurisdiction.

SECT. 2. Congress shall have power to enforce this article by appropriate legislation.

The following amendment was certified by the Secretary of State to have become valid as a part of the Constitution of the United States, July 28, 1868.

AMENDMENT 14

SECT 1. All persons born or naturalized in the United States, and subject to the jurisdiction thereof, are citizens of the United States and of the States wherein they reside. No State shall make or enforce any law which shall abridge the privileges or immunities of citizens of the United States; nor shall any State deprive any person of life, liberty, or property without due process of law; nor deny to any person within its jurisdiction the equal protection of the laws.

SECT. 2. Representatives shall be apportioned among the several States according to their respective numbers, counting the whole number of persons in each State, excluding Indians not taxed. But when the right to vote at any election for the choice of electors for President and Vice-President of the United States, representatives in Congress, the executive and judicial officers of a State, or the members of the legislature thereof, is denied to any of the male inhabitants of such State, being twenty-one years of age, and citizens of the United States, or in any way abridged, except for participation in rebellion or other crime, the basis of representation therein shall be reduced in the proportion which the number of such male citizens shall bear to the whole number of male citizens twenty-one years of age in such State.

SECT. 3. No person shall be a senator or representative in Congress, or elector of President and Vice-President, or hold any office, civil or military, under the United States, or under any State, who, having previously taken an oath as a member of Congress, or as an officer of the United States, or as a member of any State legislature, or as an executive or judicial officer of any State, to support the Constitution of the United States, shall have engaged in insurrection or rebellion against the same, or given aid or comfort to the enemies thereof. But Congress may, by a vote of two thirds of each house, remove such disability.

SECT. 4. The validity of the public debt of the United States, authorized by law, including debts incurred for payment of pensions and bounties for services in suppressing insurrection or rebellion, shall not be questioned. But neither the United States nor any State shall assume or pay any debt or obligation incurred in aid of insurrection or rebellion against the United States, or any claim for the loss or emancipation of any slave; but all such debts, obligations, and claims shall be held illegal and void.

SECT. 5. The Congress shall have power to enforce, by appropriate legislation, the provisions of this article.

The following amendment was proposed to the legislatures of the several States by the fortieth Congress, on the 27th of February, 1869, and was declared, in a proclamation of the Secretary of State, dated March 30, 1870, to have been ratified by the legislatures of twenty-nine of the thirty-seven States.

AMENDMENT 15

SECT. 1. The right of citizens of the United States to vote shall not be denied or abridged by the United States, or by any State, on account of race, color, or previous condition of servitude.

SECT. 2. Congress shall have power to enforce this article by appropriate legislation.

AMENDMENT 16

The Congress shall have the power to lay and collect taxes on incomes, from whatever source derived, without apportionment among the several States, and without regard to any census or enumeration.

AMENDMENT 17

SECT. 1. The Senate of the United States shall be composed of two Senators from each State, elected by the people thereof, for six years; and each Senator shall have one vote. The electors in each State shall have the qualifications requisite for electors of the most numerous branch of the State Legislatures.

SECT. 2. When vacancies happen in the representation of any State in the Senate, the executive authority of such State shall issue writs of election to fill such vacancies; Provided, That the Legislature of any State may empower the executive thereof to make temporary appointment until the people fill the vacancies by election as the Legislature may direct.

SECT. 3. This amendment shall not be so construed as to affect the election or term of any Senator chosen before it becomes valid as part of the Constitution.

AMENDMENT 18

SECT. 1. After one year from the ratification* of this article, the manufacture, sale, or transportation of intoxicating liquors within, the importation thereof into, or the exportation thereof

---

* Jan. 16, 1919

from the United States and all territory subject to the jurisdiction thereof, for beverage purposes, is hereby prohibited.

SECT. 2. The Congress and the several States shall have concurrent power to enforce this article by appropriate legislation.

SECT. 3. This article shall be inoperative unless it shall have been ratified as an amendment to the Constitution by the legislatures of the several States, as provided in the Constitution, within seven years from the date of the submission hereof to the States by the Congress.

AMENDMENT 19

SECT. 1. The rights of citizens of the United States to vote, shall not be denied or abridged by the United States or by any State on account of sex.

SEC. 2. Congress shall have power to enforce this article by appropriate legislation.

AMENDMENT 20

SECT. 1. The terms of the President and Vice President shall end at noon on the twentieth day of January, and the terms of Senators and Representatives at noon on the third day of January, of the years in which such terms would have ended if this article had not been ratified; and the terms of their successors shall then begin.

SECT. 2. The Congress shall assemble at least once in every year, and such meeting shall begin at noon on the third day of January, unless they shall by law appoint a different day.

SECT. 3. If, at the time fixed for the beginning of the term of the President, the President elect shall have died, the Vice President elect shall become President. If a President shall not have been chosen before the time fixed for the beginning of his term, or if the President elect shall have failed to qualify, then the Vice President elect shall act as President until a President shall have qualified; and the Congress may by law provide for the case wherein neither a President elect nor a Vice President elect shall have qualified, declaring who shall then act as President, or the manner in which one who is to act shall be selected, and such person shall act accordingly until a President or Vice President shall have qualified.

SECT. 4. The Congress may by law provide for the case of the death of any of the persons from whom the House of Representatives may choose a President whenever the right of choice shall have devolved upon them, and for the case of the death of any of the persons from whom the Senate may choose a Vice President whenever the right of choice shall have devolved upon them.

SECT. 5. Sections 1 and 2 shall take effect on the fifteenth day of October following the ratification of this article.

SECT. 6. This article shall be inoperative unless it shall have been ratified as an amendment to the Constitution by the legislatures of three-fourths of the several States within seven years from the date of its submission.

AMENDMENT 21

SECT. 1. The eighteenth article of amendment to the Constitution of the United States is hereby repealed.

SECT. 2. The transportation or importation into any State, Territory, or possession of the United States for delivery or use therein of intoxicating liquors, in violation of the laws thereof, is hereby prohibited.

SECT. 3. This article shall be inoperative unless it shall have been ratified as an amendment to the Constitution by conventions in the several States, as provided in the Constitution, within seven years from the date of the submission hereof to the States by the Congress.

AMENDMENT 22

Sect. 1. No person shall be elected to the office of the President more than twice, and no person who has held the office of President, or acted as President, for more than two years of a term to which some other person was elected President shall be elected to the office of the President more than once. But this article shall not apply to any person holding the office of the President when this article was proposed by the Congress, and shall not prevent any person who may be holding the office of President, or acting as President, during the term within which this article becomes operative from holding the office of President or acting as President during the remainder of such term.

Sect. 2. This article shall be inoperative unless it shall have been ratified as an amendment to the Constitution by the Legislatures of three-fourths of the several States within seven years from the date of its submission to the States by the Congress.

AMENDMENT 23

Sect. 1. The District constituting the seat of the Government of the United States shall appoint in such manner as the Congress may direct:

A number of electors of President and Vice President equal to the whole number of Senators and Representatives in Congress to which the District would be entitled if it were a State, but in no event more than the least populous State; they shall be in addition to those appointed by the States, but they shall be considered, for the purposes of the election of President and Vice President, to be electors appointed by a State; and they shall meet in the District and perform such duties as provided by the twelfth article of amendment.

Sect. 2. The Congress shall have power to enforce this article by appropriate legislation.

AMENDMENT 24

Sect. 1. The right of citizens of the United States to vote in any primary or other election for President or Vice President, for electors for President or Vice President, or for Senator or Representative in Congress, shall not be denied or abridged by the United States or any State by reason of failure to pay any poll tax or other tax.

Sec. 2. The Congress shall have power to enforce this article by appropriate legislation.

AMENDMENT 25

Sect. 1. In case of the removal of the President from office or of his death or resignation, the Vice President shall become President.

Sect. 2. Whenever there is a vacancy in the office of Vice President, the President shall nominate a Vice President who shall take office upon confirmation by a majority vote of both houses of Congress.

Sect. 3. Whenever the President transmits to the President pro tempore of the Senate and the Speaker of the House of Representatives his written declaration that he is unable to discharge the powers and duties of his office, and until he transmits to them a written declaration to the contrary, such powers and duties shall be discharged by the Vice President as acting President.

Sect. 4. Whenever the Vice President and a majority of either the principle officers of the executive departments or of such other body as Congress may by law provide, transmit to the President pro tempore of the Senate and the Speaker of the House of Representatives their written declaration that the President is unable to discharge the powers and duties of his office, the Vice President shall immediately assume the powers and duties of the office as Acting President.

Thereafter, when the President transmits to the President pro tempore of the Senate and the Speaker of the House of Representatives his written declaration that no inability exists, he shall resume the powers and duties of his office unless the Vice President and a majority of either the principle officers of the executive department or of such other body as Congress may by law provide, transmit within four days to the President pro tempore of the Senate and the Speaker of the House of Representatives their written declaration that the President is unable to discharge the powers and duties of his office. Thereupon Congress shall decide the issue, assembling within forty-eight hours for that purpose if not in session. If the Congress within twenty-one days after receipt of the latter written declaration, or, if Congress is required to assemble, determines by two-thirds vote of both houses that the President is unable to discharge the powers and duties of his office, the Vice President shall continue to discharge the same as Acting President; otherwise, the President shall resume the powers and duties of his office.

AMENDMENT 26

Sect. 1. The right of citizens of the United States, who are 18 years of age or older, to vote shall not be denied or abridged by the United States or any other State on account of age.

Sect. 2. The Congress shall have the power to enforce this article by appropriate legislation.

ARTICLES OF CONFEDERATION

Articles of Confederation and perpetual Union between the States of New Hampshire, Massachusetts Bay, Rhode Island and Providence Plantation, Connecticut, New York, New Jersey, Pennsylvania, Delaware, Maryland, Virginia, North Carolina, South Carolina, and Georgia.

ARTICLE I. The style of this Confederacy shall be "The United States of America."

ART. II. Each State retains its sovereignty, freedom, and independence, and every power, jurisdiction, and right, which is not by this Confederation expressly delegated to the United States in Congress assembled.

ART. III. The said States hereby severally enter into a firm league of friendship with each other, for their common defence, the security of their liberties, and their mutual and general welfare, binding themselves to assist each other against all force offered to, or attacks made upon them, or any of them, on account of religion, sovereignty, trade, or any other pretence whatever.

ART. IV. The better to secure and perpetuate mutual friendship and intercourse among the people of the different States in this Union, the free inhabitants of each of these States, paupers, vagabonds, and fugitives from justice excepted, shall be entitled to all the privileges and immunities of free citizens in the several States, and the people of each State shall have free ingress and regress to and from any other State, and shall enjoy therein all the privileges of trade and commerce, subject to the same duties, impositions, and restrictions as the inhabitants thereof respectively; provided that such restrictions shall not extend so far as to prevent the removal of property imported into any State, to any other State of which the owner is an inhabitant; provided also, that no imposition, duties, or restriction shall be laid by any State, on the property of the United States, or either of them.

If any person guilty of or charged with treason, felony, or other high misdemeanor in any State, shall flee from justice, and be found in any of the United States, he shall, upon demand of the governor or executive power of the State from which he fled, be delivered up and removed to the State having jurisdiction of his offence.

Full faith and credit shall be given in each of these States to the records, acts, and judicial proceedings of the courts and magistrates of every other State.

ART. V. For the more convenient management of the general interests of the United States, delegates shall be annually appointed in such manner as the legislature of each State shall direct, to meet in Congress on the first Monday in November, in every year, with a power reserved to each State to recall its delegates, or any of them, at any time within the year, and to send others in their stead, for the remainder of the year.

No State shall be represented in Congress by less than two, nor by more than seven members; and no person shall be capable of being a delegate for more than three years in any term of six years, nor shall any person, being a delegate, be capable of holding any office under the United States for which he or another for his benefit receives any salary, fees, or emolument of any kind.

Each State shall maintain its own delegates in a meeting of the States, and while they act as members of the committee of the States.

In determining questions in the United States, in Congress assembled, each State shall have one vote.

Freedom of speech and debate in Congress shall not be impeached or questioned in any court or place out of Congress, and the members of Congress shall be protected in their persons from arrests and imprisonments, during the time of their going to or from, and attendance on, Congress, except for treason, felony, or breach of the peace.

ART VI. No State, without the consent of the United States in Congress assembled, shall send any embassy to, or receive any embassy from, or enter into any conference, agreement, alliance, or treaty with, any king, prince, or state; nor shall any person holding any office of profit or trust under the United States, or any of them, accept of any present, emolument, office, or title of any kind whatever from any king, prince, or foreign state; nor shall the United States in Congress assembled, or any of them, grant any title of nobility.

No two or more States shall enter into any treaty, confederation, or alliance whatever between them, without the consent of the United States in Congress assembled, specifying accurately the purposes for which the same is to be entered into, and how long it shall continue.

No State shall lay any imposts or duties, which may interfere with any stipulations in treaties entered into by the United States in Congress assembled, with any king, prince, or state, in pursuance of any treaties already proposed by Congress, to the courts of France and Spain.

No vessels of war shall be kept up in time of peace by any State, except such number only as shall be deemed necessary by the United States in Congress assembled, for the defence of such State or its trade; nor shall any body of forces be kept up by any State, in time of peace, except such number only as in the judgment of the United States in Congress assembled shall be deemed requisite to garrison the forts necessary for the defence of such State; but every State shall always keep up a well regulated and disciplined militia, sufficiently armed and accoutred, and shall provide and constantly have ready for use, in public stores, a due number of field-pieces and tents, and a proper quantity of arms, ammunition and camp equipage.

No State shall engage in any war without the consent of the United States in Congress assembled, unless such State be actually invaded by enemies, or shall have received certain advice of a resolution being formed by some nation of Indians to invade such State, and the danger is so imminent as not to admit of a delay till the United States in Congress assembled can be consulted; nor shall any State grant commissions to any ships or vessels of war, nor letters of marque or reprisal, except it be after a declaration of war by the United States in Congress assembled, and then only against the kingdom or state, and the subject thereof, against which war has been so declared, and under such regulations as shall be established by the United States in Congress assembled, unless such State be infested by pirates, in which case vessels of war may be fitted out for that occasion, and kept so long as the danger shall continue, or until the United States in Congress assembled shall determine otherwise.

ART VII. When land forces are raised by any State for the common defence, all officers of or under the rank of colonel shall be appointed by the legislature of each State respectively, by whom such forces shall be raised, or in such manner as such State shall direct; and all vacancies shall be filled up by the State which first made the appointment.

ART. VIII. All charges of war and all other expenses that shall be incurred for the common defence or general welfare, and allowed by the United States in Congress assembled, shall be defrayed out of a common treasury, which shall be supplied by the several States, in proportion to the value of all land within each State, granted to or surveyed for any person, and such land and the buildings and improvements thereon shall be estimated according to such mode as the United States in Congress assembled shall from time to time direct and appoint.

The taxes for paying that proportion shall be laid and levied by the authority and direction of the legislatures of the several States within the time agreed upon by the United States in Congress assembled.

ART. IX. The United States in Congress assembled shall have the sole and exclusive right and power of determining on peace and war, except in the cases mentioned in the sixth article--of sending and receiving ambassadors--entering into treaties and alliances, provided that no treaty of commerce shall be made whereby the legislative power of the respective States shall be restrained from imposing such imposts and duties on foreigners as their own people are subjected to, or from prohibiting the exportation or importation of any species of goods or commodities whatsoever--of establishing rules for deciding, in all cases, what captures on land or water shall be legal, and in what manner prizes taken by land or naval forces in the service of the United States shall be divided or appropriated--of granting letters of marque and reprisal in time of peace--appointing courts for the trial of piracies and felonies committed on the high seas, and establishing courts for receiving and determining finally appeals in all cases of captures, provided that no member of Congress shall be appointed a judge of any of the said courts.

The United States in Congress assembled shall also be the last resort on appeal in all disputes and differences now subsisting or that hereafter may arise between two or more States concerning boundary jurisdiction, or any other cause whatever; which authority shall always be exercised in the manner following:--Whenever the legislative or executive authority or lawful agent of any State in controversy with another shall present a petition to Congress stating the matter in question and praying for a hearing, notice thereof shall be given by order of Congress to the legislative or executive authority of the other State in controversy, and a day assigned for the appearance of the parties by their lawful agents, who shall then be directed to appoint, by joint consent, commissioners or judges to constitute a court for hearing and determining the matter in question; but if they cannot agree, Congress shall name three persons out of each of the United States, and from the list of such persons each party shall alternately strike out one, the petitioners beginning, until the number shall be reduced to thirteen; and from that number not less than seven nor more than nine names, as Congress shall direct, shall, in the presence of Congress, be drawn out by lot, and the persons whose names shall be so drawn, or any five of them, shall be commissioners or judges, to hear and finally determine the controversy, so always as a major part of the judges who shall hear the cause shall agree in the determination; and if either party shall neglect to attend at the day appointed, without showing reasons, which Congress shall judge sufficient, or, being present, shall refuse to strike, the Congress shall proceed to nominate three persons out of each State, and the Secretary of Congress shall strike in behalf of such party absent or refusing; and the judgment and sentence of the court to be appointed, in the manner before prescribed, shall be final and conclusive; and if any of the parties shall refuse to submit to the authority of such court, or to appear or defend their claim or cause, the court shall nevertheless proceed to pronounce sentence or judgment, which shall in like manner be final and decisive, the judgment or sentence and other proceedings being in either case transmitted to Congress, and lodged among the acts of Congress for the security of the parties concerned: provided that every commissioner, before he sits in judgment, shall take an oath, to be administered by one of the judges of the Supreme or Superior Court of the State where the cause shall be tried, *"well and truly to hear and determine the matter in question according to the best of his judgment, without favor, affection, or hope of reward,"* provided also that no State shall be deprived of territory for the benefit of the United States.

All controversies concerning the private right of soil, claimed under different grants of two or more States, whose jurisdictions as they may respect such lands and the States which passed such grants are adjusted, the said grants or either of them being at the same time claimed to have originated antecedent to such settlement

175

of jurisdiction, shall, on the petition of either party to the Congress of the United States, be finally determined as near as may be in the same manner as is before prescribed for deciding disputes respecting territorial jurisdiction between different States.

The United States in Congress assembled shall also have the sole and exclusive right and power of regulating the alloy and value of coin struck by their own authority, or by that of the respective States--fixing the standard of weights and measures throughout the United States--regulating the trade and managing all affairs with the Indians, not members of any of the States, provided that the legislative right of any State within its own limits be not infringed or violated--establishing and regulating post-offices from one State to another, throughout all the United States, and exacting such postage on the papers passing through the same as may be requisite to defray the expenses of the said office--appointing all officers of the land forces in the service of the United States, excepting regimental officers--appointing all the officers of the naval forces, and commissioning all officers whatever in the service of the United States--making rules for the government and regulation of the said land and naval forces, and directing their operations.

The United States in Congress assembled shall have authority to appoint a committee, to sit in the recess of Congress, to be denominated "A Committee of the States," and to consist of one delegate from each State; to appoint such other committees and civil officers as may be necessary for managing the general affairs of the United States under their direction; and to appoint one of their number to preside, provided that no person be allowed to serve in the office of president more than one year in any term of three years--to ascertain the necessary sums of money to be raised for the service of the United States, and to appropriate and apply the same for defraying the public expenses--to borrow money, or emit bills on the credit of the United States, transmitting every half-year to the respective States an account of the sums of money so borrowed or emitted--to build and equip a navy--to agree upon the number of land forces, and to make requisitions from each State for its quota, in proportion to the number of white inhabitants in such State; which requisition shall be binding, and thereupon the legislature of each State shall appoint the regimental officers, raise the men, and clothe, arm, and equip them in a soldier-like manner, at the expense of the United States, and the officers and men so clothed, armed, and equipped shall march to the place appointed, and within the time agreed on by the United States in Congress assembled; but if the United States in Congress assembled shall, on consideration of circumstances, judge proper that any State should not raise men, or should raise a smaller number than its quota, and that any other State should raise a greater number of men than the quota thereof, such extra number shall be raised, officered, clothed, armed, and equipped in the same manner as the quota of such State, unless the legislature of such State shall judge that such extra number cannot be safely spared out of the same, in which case they shall raise, officer, clothe, arm, and equip as many of such extra number as they judge can be safely spared: and the officers and men, so clothed, armed, and equipped shall march to the place appointed, and within the time agreed on, by the United States in Congress assembled.

The United States in Congress assembled shall never engage in a war, nor grant letters of marque and reprisal in time of peace, nor enter into any treaties or alliances, nor coin money, nor regulate the value thereof, nor ascertain the sums and expenses necessary for the defence and welfare of the United States, or any of them, nor emit bills, nor borrow money on the credit of the United States, nor appropriate money, nor agree upon the number of vessels of war to be built or purchased, or the number of land or sea forces to be raised, nor appoint a commander-in-chief of the army or navy, unless nine States assent to the same; nor shall a question on any other point, except for adjourning from day to day, be determined, unless by the votes of a majority of the United States in Congress assembled.

The Congress of the United States shall have power to adjourn to any time within the year, and to any place within the United States, so that no period of adjournment be for a longer duration than the space of six months, and shall publish the journal of their proceedings monthly, except such parts thereof relating to treaties, alliances, or military operations, as in their judgment require secrecy, and the yeas and nays of the delegates of each State on any question shall be entered on the journal, when it is desired by any delegate; and the delegates of a State, or any of them, at his or their request, shall be furnished with a transcript of the said journal, except such parts as are above excepted, to lay before the legislatures of the several States.

ART. X. The Committee of the States, or any nine of them, shall be authorized to execute, in the recess of Congress, such of the powers of Congress as the United States in Congress assembled, by the consent of nine States, shall from time to time think expedient to vest them with: provided that no power be delegated to the said Committee, for the exercise of which, by the Articles of Confederation, the voice of nine States in the Congress of the United States assembled is requisite.

ART. XI. Canada, acceding to this Confederation, and joining in the measures of the United States, shall be admitted into and entitled to all the advantages of this Union; but no other colony shall be admitted into the same, unless such admission be agreed to by nine States.

ART. XII. All bills of credit emitted, moneys borrowed, and debts contracted by or under the authority of Congress, before the assembling of the United States in pursuance of the present Confederation, shall be deemed and considered as a charge against the United States, for payment and satisfaction whereof the said United States and the public faith are hereby solemnly pledged.

ART. XIII. Every State shall abide by the determinations of the United States in Congress assembled, on all questions which by this

Confederation are submitted to them. And the Articles of this Confederation shall be inviolably observed by every State, and the Union shall be perpetual; nor shall any alteration at any time hereafter be made in any of them, unless such alteration be agreed to in a Congress of the United States, and be afterwards confirmed by the legislatures of every State.

AND WHEREAS it hath pleased the Great Governor of the world to incline the hearts of the legislatures we respectfully represent in Congress to approve of and to authorize us to ratify the said Articles of Confederation and perpetual Union, KNOW YE, That we, the undersigned delegates, by virtue of the power and authority to us given for that purpose, do by these presents, in the name and in behalf of our respective constituents, fully and entirely ratify and confirm each and every of the said Articles of Confederation and perpetual Union, and all and singular the matters and things therein contained: and we do further solemnly plight and engage the faith of our respective constituents that they shall abide by the determinations of the United States in Congress assembled, on all questions which by the said Confederation are submitted to them. And that the Articles thereof shall be inviolably observed by the States we respectively represent, and the Union shall be perpetual.